BBC

goodfood
eatwell
LOW-FAT FEASTS

D0715669

10 9 8 7 6 5 4

BBC Books, an imprint of Ebury Publishing
20 Vauxhall Bridge Road,
London SW1V 2SA

BBC Books is part of the Penguin Random House group of companies whose addresses can be found at
global.penguinrandomhouse.com

Photographs © BBC Worldwide, 2015
Recipes © BBC Worldwide, 2015
Book design © BBC Worldwide, 2015

First published by BBC Books in 2015

www.eburypublishing.co.uk

A CIP catalogue record for this book is available from the British Library

ISBN 9781849909129

Printed and bound by Firmengruppe APPL, aprinta druck, Wemding, Germany
Colour origination by Dot Gradations Ltd, UK

Commissioning editor: Lizzy Gray
Editorial manager: Lizzy Gaisford
Project editor: Helena Caldon
Designers: Interstate Creative Partners Ltd
Design manager: Kathryn Gammon
Production: Alex Goddard

Penguin Random House is committed to a sustainable future
for our business, our readers and our planet. This book is made
from Forest Stewardship Council® certified paper.

PICTURE AND RECIPE CREDITS

BBC *Good Food* magazine and BBC Books would like to thank the following people for providing photos. While every effort has
been made to trace and acknowledge all photographers, we should like to apologize should there be any errors or omissions.

BBC Worldwide p23, p45; Chris Alack p103; Iain Bagwell p19, p117, p179; Steve Baxter p163; Clive Bozzard-Hill p159; Jean Cazals
p15; Ken Field p41, p89, p175; Will Heap p11, p37, p91, p105, p129, p145, p171; Dave King p107, p111, p147; Richard Kolker
p167; Steve Lee p73; Gareth Morgans p13, p49, p53, p67, p115, p119, p137, p157; David Munns p31, p35, p74, p99, p113, p139,
p143, p173; Myles New p39, p83, p127, p161, p187; Steve Ovenden p165, p183; Lis Parsons p177; Charlie Richards p51; Roger
Stowell p17, p21, p25, p43, p57, p59, p69, p71, p77, p81, p87, p93, p97, p101, p109, p121, p133, p135, p155, p169; Yuki Sugiura
p61; Martin Thompson p63; Simon Walton p47, p55, p79, p123, p149, p185; Philip Webb p27, p29, p33, p141; Simon Wheeler p65,
p95, p125, p131, p153; Geoff Wilkinson p151, p181

All the recipes in this book were created by the editorial team at *Good Food* and by regular contributors to BBC magazines.

BBC goodfood eatwell
LOW-FAT FEASTS

Editor **Sara Buenfeld**

BBC BOOKS

Contents
. . . .

Introduction

If you are watching your weight, keeping an eye on your cholesterol, or you just want your family to eat more healthily, this handy little book packed with brilliant recipes will be your best friend in the kitchen.

Thanks to BBC *Good Food* magazine cooking the low-fat way needn't mean sacrificing flavour. We've updated popular dishes like spaghetti Bolognese by swapping high-fat minced beef for low-fat turkey, used lean meats and skinless chicken and kept an eye on portion sizes of dairy products normally associated with saturated fat – so you can still eat well, but keep trim and healthy at the same time.

Each recipe has been analysed on a per-serving basis by a nutritional therapist, so you can see exactly what each dish contains, including the calories. To qualify for low-fat all the recipes selected in this book contain 12g fat or less per portion. But that isn't all, the calculations also separate out the saturated and unsaturated fat in each recipe, which is essential if you are wanting to control your cholesterol.

Inside the book you will discover filling soups and light meals for lunchtime, and easy-to-cook mains for every night of the week, whether you are eating meat, fish, going veggie or after something quick to make from storecupboard ingredients. There are even some guilt-free desserts for entertaining friends.

And, as always, the results are guaranteed: *Good Food* recipes are renowned in the business for being triple-tested to ensure that the recipes will work for you in your own kitchen every time.

Sara

BBC *Good Food* Magazine

Notes &
conversion tables
. . . .

NOTES ON THE RECIPES
• Eggs are large in the UK and Australia
and extra large in America unless stated.
• Wash fresh produce before preparation.
• Recipes contain nutritional analyses for
'sugar', which means the total sugar
content including all natural sugars in
the ingredients, unless otherwise stated.

OVEN TEMPERATURES

GAS	°C	°C FAN	°F	OVEN TEMP.
¼	110	90	225	Very cool
½	120	100	250	Very cool
1	140	120	275	Cool or slow
2	150	130	300	Cool or slow
3	160	140	325	Warm
4	180	160	350	Moderate
5	190	170	375	Moderately hot
6	200	180	400	Fairly hot
7	220	200	425	Hot
8	230	210	450	Very hot
9	240	220	475	Very hot

APPROXIMATE WEIGHT CONVERSIONS
• All the recipes in this book list both
metric and imperial measurements.
Conversions are approximate and
have been rounded up or down.
Follow one set of measurements
only; do not mix the two.
• Cup measurements, which are used
in Australia and America, have not
been listed here as they vary from
ingredient to ingredient. Kitchen
scales should be used to measure
dry/solid ingredients.

Good Food is concerned about
sustainable sourcing and animal
welfare. Where possible, humanely
reared meats, sustainably caught fish
(see fishonline.org for further
information from the Marine
Conservation Society) and free-range
chickens and eggs are used when
recipes are originally tested.

Spoon measurements are level unless otherwise specified.
- 1 teaspoon (tsp) = 5ml
- 1 tablespoon (tbsp) = 15ml
- 1 Australian tablespoon = 20ml (cooks in Australia should
  measure 3 teaspoons where 1 tablespoon is specified in a recipe)

APPROXIMATE LIQUID CONVERSIONS

METRIC	IMPERIAL	AUS	US
50ml	2fl oz	¼ cup	¼ cup
125ml	4fl oz	½ cup	½ cup
175ml	6fl oz	¾ cup	¾ cup
225ml	8fl oz	1 cup	1 cup
300ml	10fl oz/½ pint	½ pint	1¼ cups
450ml	16fl oz	2 cups	2 cups/1 pint
600ml	20fl oz/1 pint	1 pint	2½ cups
1 litre	35fl oz/1¾ pints	1¾ pints	1 quart

Italian vegetable soup

Vegetables and beans make this minestrone-style soup perfect for a healthy lunch or supper. For extra fibre, snap in wholewheat spaghetti in place of the pasta shapes.

 45 minutes 8

- 2 onions, chopped
- 2 carrots, chopped
- 4 celery sticks, chopped
- 1 tbsp olive or rapeseed oil
- 1 tbsp caster sugar
- 4 garlic cloves, crushed
- 2 tbsp tomato purée
- 2 bay leaves
- few thyme sprigs
- 3 courgettes, chopped
- 400g can butter beans, drained and rinsed
- 400g can chopped tomatoes
- 1.2 litres/2 pints vegetable stock
- 100g/4oz Parmesan cheese, grated
- 140g/5oz small pasta shapes
- small bunch basil, shredded
- crusty bread, to serve (optional)

1 Gently cook the onions, carrots and celery in the oil in a large pan for 20 minutes until soft. Splash in some water, if they stick. Add the sugar, garlic, tomato purée, herbs and courgettes, and cook for 4–5 minutes on a medium heat until they brown a little.

2 Tip in the beans, tomatoes and stock, then simmer for 20 minutes. Add half the cheese and the pasta and simmer for 6–8 minutes until the pasta is cooked. Sprinkle with basil and the remaining cheese and serve with hunks of crusty bread, if you like.

PER SERVING 215 kcals, protein 11g, carbs 30g, fat 6g, sat fat 3g, fibre 5g, sugar 12g, salt 1.06g

Pea & pesto soup with fish-finger croutons

A crafty way of using frozen peas and fish fingers to create a deliciously different dish.

 20 minutes 4

- 500g/1lb 2oz frozen peas
- 4 medium potatoes, peeled and cut into cubes
- 1 litre/1¾ pints hot vegetable stock
- 300g pack fish fingers (about 10)
- 3 tbsp pesto

1 Tip the peas and potatoes into a large pan, then pour in the stock. Bring to the boil and simmer for 10 minutes or until the potato chunks are tender.

2 Meanwhile, grill the fish fingers according to the pack instructions, until cooked through and golden. Cut into bite-sized cubes and keep warm.

3 Take one-third of the peas and potatoes out of the pan with a slotted spoon and set aside. Blend the rest of the soup with a hand-held blender or in a food processor until smooth, then stir in the pesto with the reserved vegetables. Heat through and serve in warm bowls with the fish-finger croutons scattered over the top.

PER SERVING 328 kcals, protein 21g, carbs 40g, fat 10g, sat fat 3g, fibre 8g, sugar 4g, salt 1.88g

Pumpkin soup

· ·

A garnish of deep-fried sage leaves provides a crisp contrast without adding too much fat. Drop dry leaves into hot oil for a few seconds until crisp, but still green.

 45 minutes 6

- 1.3kg/3lb pumpkin, peeled, sliced and deseeded
- 3 tbsp olive or rapeseed oil
- 1 large onion, chopped
- 2 garlic cloves, chopped
- 2 tsp cumin seeds
- 1 potato, peeled and chopped
- 6 thyme sprigs or 1 tsp dried
- 700ml/1¼ pints vegetable stock
- low-fat crème fraîche, to dollop
- fresh or deep-fried sage leaves, to garnish (optional)

1 Cut the pumpkin into chunks. Heat the oil in a large pan then fry the onion, garlic and cumin for 2–3 minutes. Add the pumpkin and potato and fry, stirring, for 5–6 minutes. Add the leaves from the thyme sprigs (or use dried) to the pan.

2 Pour in the stock and simmer for about 15 minutes until the pumpkin and potato are soft. Whizz in the pan with a hand blender or in a food processor until smooth. Heat through and season.

3 Serve each portion with a dollop of crème fraîche, lightly stirred in. Garnish with sage leaves and a grind of black pepper, if you like.

· ·

PER SERVING 123 kcals, protein 3g, carbs 11g, fat 6g, sat fat 1g, fibre 4g, sugar 6g, salt 0.4g

Sweet potato & lentil soup

This is a mildly spiced soup, perfect for chilly evenings. Reheat any leftovers for lunch the next day.

 40 minutes 4

- 100g/4oz red split lentils
- 1 onion, chopped
- 2 tsp olive or rapeseed oil
- 1 garlic clove, finely chopped
- 2 tbsp curry paste
- 450g/1lb sweet potatoes, peeled and cubed
- 450g/1lb floury potatoes, such as King Edward, peeled and cubed
- 1.2 litres/2 pints hot vegetable stock
- 2 tbsp chopped mint (optional)
- 142g carton low-fat natural yogurt
- warm bread, to serve

1. Cook the lentils in boiling water for 15 minutes. Fry the onion in the oil for 8 minutes until softened and beginning to brown. Stir in the garlic, curry paste and cubed potatoes. Cook for 5 minutes, stirring.
2. Drain the lentils. Add to the potatoes with the stock and simmer for 12–15 minutes until the potatoes are fully cooked. Whizz in a food processor until smooth, or straight in the pan with a hand blender. Season to taste and heat through.
3. Stir the mint, if using, into the yogurt and season to taste. Ladle the soup into bowls and swirl in the yogurt. Serve with warm bread.

PER SERVING 349 kcals, protein 13g, carbs 63g, fat 5g, sat fat 1g, fibre 9g, sugar 14g, salt 1.53kg

Cannellini-bean soup

For a prepare-ahead dinner-party starter, freeze the soup at the end of stage 2 and reheat just before serving.

 about 1 hour 6

- 1 tbsp olive or rapeseed oil
- 4 shallots, finely chopped
- 2 garlic cloves, finely chopped
- 1 carrot, finely chopped
- 2 celery sticks, finely chopped
- 2 leeks, finely chopped
- 140g/5oz streaky bacon, trimmed of fat, finely chopped
- 1.4 litres/2½ pints chicken or vegetable stock
- 2 bay leaves
- 2 tsp chopped oregano or marjoram leaves or ½ tsp dried
- 2 x 425g cans cannellini beans, drained and rinsed
- handful flat-leaf parley leaves, chopped, plus 6 sprigs to garnish
- extra virgin olive oil, to drizzle

1 Heat the oil in a large pan and tip in the shallots, garlic, carrot, celery, leeks and bacon. Cook over a medium heat for 5–7 minutes, stirring occasionally, until softened but not browned.

2 Pour in the stock, then add the bay leaves and oregano or marjoram. Season and bring to the boil, then cover the pan and simmer gently for 15 minutes. Tip in the beans, cover again and simmer for a further 5 minutes.

3 To serve, taste for seasoning and swirl in the chopped parsley. Ladle into warm bowls and top each with a drizzle of extra virgin olive oil and a parsley sprig.

PER SERVING 203 kcals, protein 10g, carbs 19g, fat 9g, sat fat 2g, fibre 5g, sugar 6g, salt 1.78g

Vegetable & pesto soup

A simple soup that allows the flavour of fresh summer vegetables to shine through. If you want to cut the fat content further, use a reduced-fat pesto.

 30 minutes 4

- 1 tbsp olive or rapeseed oil
- 1 onion, chopped
- 225g/8oz new potatoes, sliced
- 1 vegetable stock cube
- 100g/4oz runner beans, sliced
- 450g/1lb courgettes, sliced then halved
- 2–3 tbsp pesto

1 Heat the oil in a large pan and fry the onion for 8 minutes until golden. Add the potato slices and mix well. Dissolve the stock cube in 1.2 litres/2 pints boiling water, then add to the pan. Bring to the boil then simmer for 7 minutes until the potatoes are just cooked.

2 Add the runner beans to the pan and continue to cook for 5 minutes, adding the courgettes for the last 2 minutes of cooking time.

3 Season with plenty of salt and black pepper. Remove from the heat and stir in 2 tablespoons of the pesto. Taste and add more pesto if necessary and grind over some black pepper. Serve hot.

PER SERVING 160 kcals, protein 4g, carbs 16g, fat 9g, sat fat 1g, fibre 3g, sugar 5g, salt 1.54g

Asian vegetable broth

Vary the combination of vegetables to suit yourself; even a bag of prepared stir-fry vegetables from the supermarket or freezer would do.

 20 minutes   4

- 1 lemongrass stalk, thinly sliced
- 2.5cm/1in piece ginger, sliced
- 2 garlic cloves, sliced
- 4 tbsp light soy sauce
- 2 tbsp saké or dry sherry
- finely grated zest and juice 1 lime
- 1 tsp caster sugar
- 2 tbsp vegetable or rapeseed oil
- 2 carrots, cut into matchsticks
- 100g/4oz baby corn, halved
- 1 large red chilli, deseeded and sliced
- 100g/4oz oyster mushrooms, sliced
- 50g/2oz baby leaf spinach
- 85g/3oz beansprouts

1 Put the lemongrass, ginger and garlic in a large pan with the soy sauce, saké or sherry, lime zest and juice and caster sugar. Add 850ml/1½ pints water and bring to the boil. Cover and simmer for 10 minutes. Strain and keep the broth warm.
2 Heat the oil in a large frying pan or wok, add the carrots, corn and chilli, and stir-fry for 2 minutes. Add the mushrooms, spinach and beansprouts, and remove from the heat.
3 Divide the vegetables among four serving bowls, pour over the hot broth and serve immediately.

PER SERVING 130 kcals, protein 4g, carbs 9g, fat 8g, sat fat 1g, fibre 3g, sugar 1g, salt 2.3g

Meal-in-a-bowl noodle soup

When you are hungry and in a hurry this meal for one is perfect. Look for fresh Japanese udon or yakisoba noodles in the ethnic section of the supermarket.

 15 minutes    1 (easily doubled)

- 1 tsp vegetable or rapeseed oil
- 5 mushrooms, sliced
- 2 garlic cloves, finely chopped
- 1 tsp grated ginger
- ½ red pepper, deseeded and cut into strips
- small stalk broccoli, broken into florets
- 1 tbsp reduced-salt soy sauce
- 1 tbsp tomato ketchup
- 1 tsp Worcestershire sauce
- 150g pack straight-to-wok thick udon noodles

1 Heat the oil in a medium pan. Add the mushrooms, garlic, ginger, red pepper and broccoli and stir-fry until the vegetables are beginning to soften, about 4 minutes.

2 Meanwhile, stir the soy, ketchup and Worcestershire sauce into 300ml/½ pint boiling water. Pour into the pan and add the noodles.

3 Cook the noodles for 2 minutes until they are tender and piping hot, then ladle the soup into a bowl to serve.

PER SERVING 156 kcals, protein 8g, carbs 18g, fat 4g, sat fat 1g, fibre 6g, sugar 14g, salt 2.6g

Smoked-haddock chowder

To give this simple, healthy soup a kick, add a dash of Tabasco sauce, if you like.

 20-25 minutes  2

- 1 onion, chopped
- 2 potatoes, scrubbed and sliced
- 500ml/18fl oz vegetable stock
- 2 skinless smoked haddock fillets, about 100g/4oz each, cut into chunks
- 418g can creamed corn
- skimmed milk, to taste
- handful flat-leaf parsley, chopped

1 Put the onion and potatoes into a large pan. Pour over the vegetable stock and simmer for 6–8 minutes until the potatoes are soft, but still have a slight bite. Add the chunks of smoked haddock. Tip in the creamed corn and add a little milk if you like a thick chowder, more if you like it thinner.

2 Gently simmer the chowder for 5–7 minutes until the haddock is cooked (it should flake when cut with a fork). Sprinkle over the parsley and ladle the chowder into bowls.

PER SERVING 431 kcals, protein 28g, carbs 70g, fat 3g, sat fat 0.1g, fibre 7g, sugar 18g, salt 3.3g

Moroccan chickpea soup

A tasty vegetable dish, but meat-lovers may like to fry two sliced chorizo sausages with the onion and celery. For extra spice, add a little harissa paste.

 20–25 minutes 4

- 1 tbsp olive or rapeseed oil
- 1 medium onion, chopped
- 2 celery sticks, chopped
- 2 tsp ground cumin
- 600ml/1 pint vegetable stock
- 400g can chopped tomatoes with garlic
- 400g can chickpeas, drained and rinsed
- 100g/4oz frozen broad beans
- juice and grated zest ½ lemon
- large handful coriander or parsley leaves
- warm coriander naan, to serve

1 Heat the oil in a large pan, then fry the onion and celery gently for 10 minutes until softened, stirring frequently. Tip in the cumin and fry for another minute.

2 Turn up the heat, then add the stock, tomatoes and chickpeas, plus a good grind of black pepper. Simmer for 8 minutes. Throw in the broad beans and lemon juice, and cook for a further 2 minutes.

3 Season to taste, then top with a sprinkling of lemon zest and chopped herbs. Serve with warm coriander naan.

PER SERVING 153 kcals, protein 9g, carbs 18g, fat 5g, sat fat 1g, fibre 7g, sugar 6g, salt 1.07g

Roast asparagus with garlic

To prepare asparagus, bend the spears and you will notice a woody section at the bottom of the spear. Snap this off and they are ready to cook.

🕐 20 minutes   🥧 4, as a starter

- 350g/12oz asparagus
- 2 tbsp olive or rapeseed oil
- 1 large garlic clove, cut into very thin slices
- 1 tbsp large capers in brine, drained and rinsed
- juice ½ orange

1 Heat oven to 200C/180C fan/gas 6. Bring a large pan of water to the boil. Add the asparagus and boil for 2 minutes until crisp, but beginning to go tender.

2 Drain and refresh under cold water. Dry on kitchen paper. Pour the oil into a shallow roasting tin and roll the asparagus in it to coat.

3 Scatter over the garlic slivers and the capers, and roast for 8–10 minutes until the asparagus is tinged browned and cooked through – test by inserting a knife into a few spears. Sprinkle with orange juice, season with sea salt and serve warm.

PER SERVING 78 kcals, protein 3g, carbs 3g, fat 6g, sat fat 1g, fibre 2g, sugar 2g, salt 0.2g

Chicken livers on toast

Most often used in pâtés and stuffings, chicken livers are also delicious pan-fried and served on toast as a starter or light lunch. They're great value for money too.

 30 minutes 4

- 250g/9oz chicken livers
- 2 shallots, finely chopped
- large handful flat-leaf parsley, leaves very roughly chopped
- 1 tbsp capers, drained and rinsed, roughly chopped
- 2 tbsp olive or rapeseed oil
- 3 tbsp sherry vinegar
- 4 slices good-quality bread, such as sourdough
- 1 tbsp plain flour
- large pinch cayenne pepper

1 Pick over the livers, cutting away any fatty bits and sinew, then pat them dry. Put the shallots, parsley and capers into a bowl, and drizzle with half the olive oil and 1 tablespoon of the vinegar then set aside.

2 Toast the bread (preferably on a griddle but a toaster is fine). Toss the livers in the flour and cayenne pepper, and season generously. Heat the rest of the oil in a frying pan and fry the livers over a really high heat for 4–5 minutes until brown and crisp on the outside and cooked, but still a little pink in the middle. Splash the remaining vinegar into the pan and bubble down for 1 minute.

3 Tip the contents of the pan in with the shallot mix. Toss everything together, season to taste, then pile on to the toasted bread – there is no need to butter it. Season with a little salt and serve.

PER SERVING 221 kcals, protein 14g, carbs 25g, fat 8g, sat fat 1g, fibre 2g, sugar 1g, salt 0.83g

Baked buttery squash

Butternut squash has a lovely sweet, rich flavour. In fact, this recipe has a buttery taste without being high in fat.

 1 hour 10 minutes   2

- 1 butternut squash, about 675g/1lb 8oz total
- ½ tsp paprika
- 3 tbsp snipped chives
- 3 tbsp low-fat crème fraîche
- 1 thick slice white bread, crust removed, crumbled into breadcrumbs
- generous knob butter, melted
- 25g/1oz grated Parmesan
- crisp green salad, to serve

1 Heat oven to 200C/180C fan/gas 6. Halve the squash lengthways, then scoop out and discard the seeds and fibres. Season the squash well and put in a roasting tin half-full of water. Cover with foil and bake for about 40 minutes until tender.

2 Drain, then transfer the squash to a board until cool enough to handle. Scrape the flesh into a bowl, leaving a thin border of flesh on the skin. Mix the paprika, chives and crème fraîche with the flesh and season.

3 Pile the mixture into the squash shells. Mix the breadcrumbs with the butter and Parmesan, and sprinkle on top. Bake for 15 minutes until lightly browned. Serve with a crisp green salad.

PER SERVING 282 kcals, protein 13g, carbs 35g, fat 10g, sat fat 6g, fibre 7g, sugar 14g, salt 0.78g

Seeded-bagel tuna melts

A really quick and healthy bagel idea that's perfect as a snack or light lunch.

 10 minutes 4

- 4 mixed seed bagels
- 200g can tuna in spring water, drained
- 1 tbsp mayonnaise
- juice 1 lemon
- 1 bunch spring onions, roughly chopped
- 2 tomatoes, sliced
- handful grated mature reduced-fat Cheddar

1 Heat the grill to high. Split open the bagels, lay them on a baking sheet, then toast both sides until golden.
2 Meanwhile, tip the tuna into a bowl and add the mayonnaise, lemon juice and spring onions. Season to taste and mix well.
3 Spread the tuna mix over the bottom half of each of the 4 bagels and top with tomato slices. Sprinkle over the handful of grated Cheddar, then grill for 1 minute or until melted. Finish with the bagel tops and serve.

PER BAGEL 257 kcals, protein 17g, carbs 29g, fat 9g, sat fat 3g, fibre 2g, sugar 4g, salt 1.28g

Jackets with tuna & chives

· ·

Don't let the lengthy cooking time put you off. The actual work takes only 10 minutes; the hard work is all done in the oven!.

 1½ hours   4

- 4 small baking potatoes
- 250g tub virtually fat-free cottage cheese with onions and chives
- 200g can good-quality tuna in spring water, drained
- 1 celery stick, sliced
- 3 spring onions, trimmed and sliced
- Tabasco sauce, to sprinkle
- green salad, to serve

1 Heat oven to 180C/160C fan/gas 4. Prick the potatoes with a fork. Put them straight on to a shelf in the hottest part of the oven for 1–1¼ hours, or until they are soft inside.
2 Meanwhile, mix the cottage cheese with the tuna, celery and spring onions to make the filling. Season.
3 To serve, cut a deep cross in each baked potato and spoon the filling on top. Sprinkle a few drops of Tabasco sauce over and serve with a green salad.

· ·
PER SERVING 232 kcals, protein 20g, carbs 32g, fat 1g, sat fat none, fibre 4g, sugar 3g, salt 0.61g

Trout, beetroot & bean salad

· ·

A good-looking salad, and good for you too. Horseradish is delicious with both trout and beetroot.

 15 minutes   4

- 225g/8oz fine green beans, trimmed
- 120g bag watercress and rocket salad
- 2 tsp balsamic vinegar
- 250g pack cooked smoked trout fillets
- 4 cooked beetroot, diced
- 6 tbsp 0% fat fromage frais
- 1–2 tbsp lemon juice
- 2 tsp creamed horseradish

1 Cook the green beans in a pan of lightly salted boiling water for 3–4 minutes until just tender. Drain and refresh in cold water.
2 Put the salad leaves in a large bowl and season. Pour in the balsamic vinegar and toss well to coat. Arrange the dressed leaves in a serving dish. Flake the trout on to the leaves and top with the cooked beans and diced beetroot.
3 Mix the fromage frais, lemon juice and creamed horseradish in a small bowl, and season to taste. Drizzle over the salad just before serving.

· ·
PER SERVING 138 kcals, protein 17g, carbs 8g, fat 4g, sat fat 1g, fibre 4g, sugar 6g, salt 1.52g

Tuna, bean & corn salad

Not just quick to do, this easy salad is made from storecupboard ingredients, so there's no shopping either!

🕐 10 minutes 📊 2 (easily doubled)

- 125g can tuna slices or 185g can tuna chunks in spring water, drained
- 165g can sweetcorn with peppers, drained
- ½ red onion, finely chopped
- 200g can red kidney beans, drained and rinsed
- 2 handfuls mixed salad leaves
- 1 tbsp olive or rapeseed oil
- 2 tsp lemon juice
- pinch mild chilli powder
- toasted crusty bread, to serve

1 In a large bowl, mix the tuna lightly with the sweetcorn, onion and kidney beans. Season well.
2 Divide the salad leaves between two plates, season lightly, then pile the tuna salad on top.
3 Drizzle over the oil and lemon juice, and sprinkle with the chilli. Serve with toasted crusty bread.

PER SERVING 277 kcals, protein 21g, carbs 33g, fat 8g, sat fat 1g, fibre 6g, sugar 5g, salt 1.63g

Japanese salad with rice

A simple salad of crunchy vegetables in a warm dressing, served with sticky sushi rice.

 20 minutes, plus standing 4

- 225g/8oz sushi rice
- 1 mooli (large white radish), peeled
- 2 carrots, peeled
- 1 small cucumber (about 250g/9oz)
- 3 tbsp mirin (Japanese sweet rice wine) or dry sherry
- 2 tbsp rice wine vinegar
- 2 tbsp soy sauce
- 2 tsp caster sugar
- coriander sprigs, to garnish

1 Rinse the rice in a sieve in cold water until the water runs clear. Put the rice in a pan and pour over 300ml/½ pint cold water, cover, then bring to the boil. Simmer for 10 minutes without removing the lid. Leave to stand, covered, for 10 minutes.

2 Meanwhile, cut the mooli, carrots and cucumber into matchsticks and put in a bowl. Put the remaining ingredients in a small pan and heat gently until steam starts to rise. Pour the hot marinade over the vegetables and marinate for 15 minutes.

3 Divide the rice among four serving plates, spoon the vegetables on top, then drizzle the marinade over. Serve immediately, topped with the coriander.

PER SERVING 254 kcals, protein 5g, carbs 57g, fat 1g, sat fat 0.03g, fibre 1g, sugar 3g, salt 1.15g

Warm potato & spinach salad

This bistro salad is packed with interesting textures and flavours from the beans, crispy bacon and vegetables.

 30 minutes 4

- 700g/1lb 9oz new potatoes, scrubbed and halved
- 225g bag baby leaf spinach
- 4 rashers smoked back bacon, trimmed of fat
- 175g/6oz button mushrooms, thinly sliced
- 410g can butter beans, drained and rinsed

FOR THE DRESSING
- 1 garlic clove, crushed
- 2 tsp wholegrain mustard
- 2 tsp balsamic vinegar
- 1 tbsp olive or rapeseed oil

1 Cook the potatoes in salted boiling water for 8–10 minutes until just tender. Drain and immediately toss with the spinach leaves so they wilt very slightly. Set aside.

2 Heat grill to high. Grill the bacon for 5–6 minutes until the rashers are very crisp. Drain on kitchen paper and chop roughly into pieces when cool. Mix all the dressing ingredients in a large bowl. Add the mushrooms and butter beans, season and leave to stand for 5 minutes.

3 Add the potatoes, spinach and bacon pieces to the mushrooms and butter beans, then toss together. Serve at once.

PER SERVING 280 kcals, protein 13g, carbs 39g, fat 8g, sat fat 2g, fibre 7g, sugar 4g, salt 1.94g

Hoisin wraps

Hoisin sauce keeps well in the fridge and can be used to turn leftover chicken or turkey into a tasty snack like this.

 10 minutes 2

- 200g/7oz cooked turkey or chicken, cut into strips
- 4 tbsp hoisin sauce
- 2 flour tortillas
- ½ cucumber, deseeded and shredded
- 4 spring onions, trimmed and finely shredded
- good handful watercress

1 Heat grill to high. Mix the turkey or chicken with half of the hoisin sauce so that it's coated, then spread over an ovenproof dish and grill until sizzling. Set aside and keep warm.
2 Warm the tortillas under the grill, or according to the pack instructions.
3 Spread the tortillas with the rest of the hoisin sauce, add the turkey or chicken with the cucumber, onions and watercress, and wrap up the whole lot. Cut in half and enjoy while still warm.

PER WRAP 302 kcals, protein 33g, carbs 31g, fat 6g, sat fat 1g, fibre 2g, sugar 12g, salt 1.81g

Pumpkin-falafel pockets

These little patties are delicious in pitta bread with the carrot and feta salad, and make a nutritious veggie meal. Up the amount of chilli, if you like things spicy.

 50 minutes, plus chilling 4

- 1kg/2lb 4oz pumpkin or butternut squash, deseeded and cut into wedges
- 400g can chickpeas, drained, rinsed and dried
- 1 garlic clove, chopped
- ½ tsp chilli flakes
- 1 tsp ground cumin
- small bunch parsley leaves, roughly chopped
- 2 slices white or wholemeal bread, whizzed to crumbs
- 4 wholemeal pitta breads, to serve

FOR THE SALAD
- 2 carrots, coarsely grated
- ½ small red onion, finely sliced
- 100g/4oz feta, crumbled

1 Put the pumpkin or squash in a microwave-safe bowl and cover with cling film. Cook on High for 10 minutes or until soft.

2 Meanwhile, tip the chickpeas, garlic, chilli flakes, cumin and half the parsley into a food processor, then whizz until the chickpeas are finely chopped but not smooth.

3 Allow the pumpkin or squash to cool slightly, then scoop the flesh from the skin and add to the chickpea mix with some seasoning and the breadcrumbs. Give everything a good stir, then shape the mixture into 12 little patties or falafels with your hands. Put the falafels on a plate and chill for 10 minutes.

4 Heat grill to medium. Meanwhile, mix the remaining parsley with the salad ingredients. Put the falafels on a baking sheet and grill for 3–5 minutes on each side. Split the pitta breads lengthways and fill with the warm falafels and some of the feta salad.

PER POCKET 346 kcals, protein 17g, carbs 54g, fat 8g, sat fat 4g, fibre 9g, sugar 9g, salt 1.91g

Chickpea & coriander burgers

A healthy low-fat, high-fibre veggie alternative to the classic burger. The recipe can easily be doubled, and the burgers can be frozen uncooked or cooked.

 30 minutes 4

- 400g can chickpeas, drained and rinsed
- zest 1 lemon, plus juice ½
- 1 tsp ground cumin
- small bunch coriander, ½ chopped
- 1 egg
- 100g/4oz fresh breadcrumbs
- 1 medium red onion, ½ diced, ½ sliced
- 1 tbsp olive or rapeseed oil
- 4 small wholemeal buns
- 1 large tomato, sliced
- ½ cucumber, sliced
- few dollops chilli sauce

1 In a food processor, whizz the chickpeas, lemon zest and juice, cumin, chopped coriander, egg and some seasoning. Scrape the mix into a bowl and stir in 85g/3oz of the breadcrumbs and the diced onion. Form the mixture into four burgers, press the remaining breadcrumbs on to both sides and chill.

2 Heat the oil in a frying pan until hot. Fry the burgers for 4 minutes on each side, keeping the heat on medium so they don't burn. To serve, slice each bun and fill with a burger, some sliced onion, tomato and cucumber, a dollop of chilli sauce and the remaining coriander.

PER SERVING 344 kcals, protein 15g, carbs 56g, fat 8g, sat fat 1g, fibre 6g, sugar 6g, salt 1.30g

Spicy Thai fish kebabs

Unlike some Thai dishes, these tasty kebabs are not too hot, just mildly spicy.

 20–30 minutes   2

- 1 tsp vegetable or rapeseed oil, plus extra to grease
- 1 tbsp Thai lemongrass and coconut stir-fry seasoning
- 250g/9oz skinless plaice or pollack fillets, cut into long strips
- 1 yellow pepper, deseeded and cut into chunks
- 1 onion, cut into chunks
- 4 cherry tomatoes
- Thai jasmine rice, to serve

FOR THE DIP
- 1 tbsp chopped parsley
- 150g/5oz low-fat natural yogurt
- lemon juice, to taste

1 Heat oven to 180C/160C fan/gas 4. Line a baking sheet with foil and brush lightly with oil.

2 Mix the Thai seasoning and oil in a shallow bowl and season well. Roll the fish in the spice mixture, then loosely concertina it on four skewers (pre-soaked, if wooden). Follow with two to three chunks of pepper and onion per skewer, and finish with a cherry tomato.

3 Roast the skewers on the foil for 8–10 minutes or until the fish is white and opaque. Stir the parsley for the dip into the yogurt in a small bowl, then add the lemon juice and some seasoning to taste. Serve the dip with the kebabs and rice.

PER SERVING 241 kcals, protein 27g, carbs 18g, fat 7g, sat fat 1g, fibre 4g, sugar 15g, salt 2.07g

Tomato & olive spaghetti

Take a few storecupboard basics and you can have supper on the table in 15 minutes.

 15 minutes 4

- 350g/12oz spaghetti
- 1 tbsp olive or rapeseed oil
- 2 garlic cloves, finely chopped
- 4 anchovy fillets in oil, drained
- 400g can plum tomatoes
- 100g/4oz pitted black olives, roughly chopped
- 3 tbsp capers, rinsed and roughly chopped
- 2 tbsp chopped flat-leaf parsley leaves

1 Stir the spaghetti into a large pan of salted boiling water and cook for 12–15 minutes until just tender.
2 Meanwhile, heat the oil in a pan and cook the garlic and anchovies for 2 minutes. Tip in the tomatoes and cook for 5 minutes, breaking them lightly with a wooden spoon. Stir in the olives and capers and cook for a further 5 minutes. Season to taste and stir in the parsley.
3 Drain the pasta well and return to the pan. Stir in the sauce, divide among warmed bowls and serve.

PER SERVING 377 kcals, protein 13g, carbs 68g, fat 8g, sat fat 1g, fibre 4g, sugar 6g, salt 2.3g

Seafood spaghetti

There's more to spaghetti than Bolognese. Try this low-fat sauce made with a jar of cockles.

 15 minutes   2

- 175g/6oz spaghetti
- 1 tbsp olive or rapeseed oil
- 2 garlic cloves, finely chopped
- 400g can chopped tomatoes
- 200g jar cockles in vinegar, drained
- pinch dried chilli flakes
- 2 tbsp chopped flat-leaf parsley leaves

1 Cook the spaghetti in a pan of salted boiling water for 10–12 minutes until tender.
2 Meanwhile, heat the oil in a frying pan then fry the garlic for 30 seconds. Add the tomatoes and bubble for 2–3 minutes. Add the cockles and chilli flakes, season, then stir to heat through.
3 Drain the spaghetti and return to the pan. Stir in the sauce and serve sprinkled with chopped parsley.

PER SERVING 424 kcals, protein 21g, carbs 71g, fat 8g, sat fat 1g, fibre 5g, sugar 8g, salt 1.39g

Tagliatelle with vegetable ragu

· · · · · · · · · · · · · · · · · · · ·

This low-fat ragu is easily doubled so you can freeze some for another day. Add
chilli powder and canned kidney beans for a terrific chilli to serve with rice.

 50 minutes   5

- 1 onion, finely chopped
- 2 celery sticks, finely chopped
- 2 carrots, diced
- 4 garlic cloves, crushed
- 1 tbsp tomato purée
- 1 tbsp balsamic vinegar
- 250g/9oz diced vegetables, such as courgettes, peppers and mushrooms
- 50g/2oz red split lentils
- 2 x 400g cans chopped tomatoes with basil
- 250g/9oz tagliatelle (or your favourite pasta)
- 2 tbsp shaved Parmesan cheese (optional)

1 Tip the onion, celery and carrots into a large non-stick pan and add 2–3 tablespoons water, or stock if you have some. Cook gently, stirring often, until the vegetables are soft.

2 Add the garlic, tomato purée and balsamic vinegar, and cook on a high heat for 1 minute more. Add the diced veg, lentils and tomatoes, then bring to the boil. Lower to a simmer, then cook the ragu for about 20 minutes.

3 Meanwhile, cook the pasta according to the pack instructions, then drain. Season the ragu and serve with the pasta and some cheese on top, if you like.

· ·
PER SERVING 321 kcals, protein 15g, carbs 55g, fat 3g, sat fat 2g, fibre 5g, sugar 12g, salt 0.3g

Spaghetti with broccoli & anchovies

If you love garlic, try adding a couple of chopped cloves to the breadcrumbs. Garlic is well known for helping to reduce cholesterol.

 25–30 minutes   4

- 350g/12oz spaghetti
- 350g/12oz broccoli
- 3–4 tbsp olive or rapeseed oil
- 6 anchovy fillets in oil, drained and chopped
- 2 red chillies, deseeded and finely chopped
- 100g/4oz white breadcrumbs, made with stale bread

1 Cook the spaghetti in a large pan of boiling water, according to the pack instructions. Cut the broccoli into small florets, thinly slicing the thick stalks, and throw into the pan of pasta for the last 3 minutes of cooking time.

2 Meanwhile, heat 3 tablespoons of the oil in a frying pan, add the anchovies and chillies, and fry briefly. Add the breadcrumbs and cook, stirring, for about 5 minutes until the crumbs are crunchy and golden.

3 Drain the spaghetti and return to the pan. Toss with three-quarters of the crumb mixture, some salt and pepper and another tablespoon of the oil, if you like. Serve each portion sprinkled with the remaining crumbs.

PER SERVING 480 kcals, protein 17g, carbs 78g, fat 11g, sat fat 2g, fibre 5g, sugar 5g, salt 0.8g

Creamy tomato & pepper pasta

This is excellent for using up soft tomatoes. The creaminess comes from the crème fraîche; we've use a reduced-fat version, which you should be careful not to overheat.

 50 minutes 4

- 900g/2lb ripe tomatoes
- 1 red pepper
- 2 garlic cloves
- 2 tbsp olive or rapeseed oil
- 350g/12oz pasta quills or shells
- 4 tbsp half-fat crème fraîche
- grated Parmesan, to serve

1 Heat oven to 200C/180C fan/gas 6. Quarter the tomatoes, roughly chop the pepper (discarding the seeds) and finely chop the garlic. Put the veg in a roasting tin and drizzle over the oil. Season well.

2 Roast for 30–35 minutes, stirring halfway through, until softened and slightly browned. Meanwhile, cook the pasta in a large pan of salted boiling water for 10–12 minutes until just tender.

3 Remove the vegetables from the oven and stir in the crème fraîche a spoonful at a time. Gently reheat on the stove, taste and season if necessary. Stir in the drained pasta and serve with grated Parmesan.

PER SERVING 440 kcals, protein 13g, carbs 71g, fat 10g, sat fat 3g, fibre 4g, sugar 12g, salt 0.38g

Spaghetti with tomato, chilli & tuna salsa

· ·

Not just low fat, this satisfying supper for the family can also be thrown together quickly, if you are short of time.

 20 minutes 4

- 350g/12oz spaghetti
- 1 small red onion
- 500g/1lb 2oz tomatoes
- 2 tbsp olive or rapeseed oil
- 1 red chilli, deseeded and chopped
- 140g can tuna in brine, drained

1 Cook the spaghetti in plenty of boiling salted water, according to the pack instructions.

2 Meanwhile, finely chop the onion and tomatoes, and put them in a large pan along with the oil. Add the chilli to the pan. Gently heat through for a few minutes, stirring well.

3 Drain the pasta and add to the sauce, then break up the tuna and add to the pan. Season to taste, then toss well and serve in bowls.

· ·

PER SERVING 404 kcals, protein 18g, carbs 70g, fat 8g, sat fat 1g, fibre 4g, sugar 8g, salt 0.52g

Spring-vegetable tagliatelle with lemon sauce

This pasta dish, topped with the new season's spring veg, looks and tastes good enough for a casual supper with friends.

 30 minutes 4

- 450g/1lb mixed spring vegetables, including green beans, asparagus, broad beans, peas
- 400g/14oz tagliatelle
- juice 1 lemon, zest ½
- 1 tbsp Dijon mustard
- 1 tbsp olive or rapeseed oil
- 3 tbsp snipped chives
- shaved Parmesan cheese, to serve

1 Halve the green beans and cut the asparagus into three pieces on the diagonal. Cook the tagliatelle according to the pack instructions, adding the mixed vegetables for the final 5 minutes of the cooking time.

2 Meanwhile, put the lemon juice in a small pan with the mustard, oil and a little black pepper. Warm through, stirring until smooth.

3 Drain the pasta and veg; add 4 tablespoons of the cooking water to the lemon sauce. Return the pasta and veg to the pan, reheat the sauce, adding most of the chives, then add to the pasta mix, tossing everything together well. Divide among four shallow bowls and top each with a grinding of black pepper, a few shavings of cheese and the remaining chives.

PER SERVING 469 kcals, protein 21g, carbs 84g, fat 8g, sat fat 3g, fibre 7g, sugar 4g, salt 0.48g

Roast tomato & pepper gnocchi

Tangy goat's cheese goes wonderfully with the smoky peppers. Try it with spaghetti or pasta shapes too.

 25 minutes 4

- 450g/1lb ripe tomatoes, halved
- 2 red peppers, deseeded and cut into strips
- 2 garlic cloves, unpeeled
- 1½ tbsp olive or rapeseed oil
- 500g pack fresh gnocchi
- 100g/4oz goat's cheese
- basil leaves, to garnish
- green salad, to serve

1 Heat oven to 220C/200C fan/gas 7. Put the tomatoes, peppers, garlic and oil in a roasting tin. Sprinkle with salt and stir to coat. Roast for 20 minutes. Just before the tomatoes and peppers are done, cook the gnocchi in salted boiling water for 2–3 minutes or according to the pack instructions.

2 Remove the tomatoes, peppers and garlic from the oven. Squeeze the garlic from its skin and put in a food processor with the tomatoes, peppers and pan juices. Season. Whizz for a few seconds for a rough sauce.

3 Drain the gnocchi and transfer to a bowl. Pour the sauce over the gnocchi and mix gently. Divide among plates, crumble over the cheese and tear over the basil leaves. Serve with a green salad.

PER SERVING 329 kcals, protein 10g, carbs 44g, fat 11g, sat fat 5g, fibre 5g, sugar 10g, salt 1.4g

Fragrant rice with chilli vegetables

Simple ingredients are given a flavour boost with fresh-tasting lemongrass, coriander and the fiery heat of chopped chilli.

 45 minutes   4

- 225g/8oz jasmine or Thai rice
- 1 lemongrass stalk, finely chopped
- 175g/6oz mangetout, halved lengthways
- 175g/6oz baby sweetcorn, halved lengthways
- 2 tomatoes, roughly chopped
- 25g/1oz coriander leaves, finely chopped
- 25g/1oz desiccated coconut, lightly toasted
- 1 red chilli, deseeded and finely chopped
- 1 tbsp light soy sauce
- coriander sprigs, to garnish

1 Half-fill the base of a steamer with water. Bring to the boil and cover with the steamer layer and lid. Rinse the rice under cold running water. Drain and put into a basin (check it will fit into the steamer layer). Add the lemongrass, some seasoning and 600ml/ 1 pint boiling water to the basin. Put into the steamer and put on the lid. Cook for 30 minutes until the rice has absorbed almost all the water.

2 Arrange the vegetables in the steamer, around the basin. Cover and steam for 2 minutes.

3 Stir the coriander, coconut and chilli into the rice and divide the rice among serving plates. Top with the vegetables and drizzle over the soy sauce. Serve sprinkled with the coriander sprigs.

PER SERVING 249 kcals, protein 7g, carbs 48g, fat 5g, sat fat 3g, fibre 3g, sugar 3g, salt 0.65g

Tuna & tomato rice

Many kids who don't like fish will eat tuna, especially in a tasty all-in-one meal like this.

 25 minutes 4

- 225g/8oz long grain rice
- 1 tbsp olive or rapeseed oil
- 2 garlic cloves, finely chopped
- 1 onion, finely chopped
- 2 smoked streaky bacon rashers, trimmed of fat, chopped
- 175g/6oz chestnut mushrooms, sliced
- 2 x 400g cans chopped tomatoes
- 200g can tuna in spring water, drained
- generous handful flat-leaf parsley leaves, finely chopped

1 Cook the rice in salted boiling water for 10–12 minutes, or according to the pack instructions.

2 Meanwhile, heat the oil in a pan and fry the garlic, onion and bacon for 5 minutes, stirring often. Add the mushrooms and cook for another 2–3 minutes. Stir in the tomatoes and tuna, and season well. Heat through for 5 minutes.

3 Drain the rice, stir it into the tomato sauce with the parsley, mixing gently, then divide among four bowls to serve.

PER SERVING 346 kcals, protein 19g, carbs 57g, fat 6g, sat fat 2g, fibre 6g, sugar 3g, salt 3.52g

Quick fish risotto

Use your microwave to make perfect rice in next to no time. You'll easily find risotto rice in the supermarket.

 20 minutes 4

- 1 onion, finely chopped
- 1 garlic clove, finely chopped
- 1 vegetable or fish stock cube
- 250g/9oz risotto rice
- 250g/9oz smoked cod or haddock, skinned and cut into chunks
- large cupful frozen peas
- knob butter
- 1 lemon, cut into 8 wedges, to garnish

1 Put the onion and garlic in a large heatproof non-metallic bowl with the stock cube and 300ml/½ pint boiling water. Stir well, then cover and microwave on High for 3 minutes.

2 Stir in the rice with another 300ml/½ pint boiling water, cover and microwave on High for 10 minutes, stirring after 5 minutes.

3 Stir the fish into the rice with the peas and another 300ml/½ pint boiling water. Cover and microwave on High for 4 minutes. Check the rice is cooked – if not, cook for another minute. Leave to stand for 1–2 minutes for the liquid to be absorbed. Stir in the butter and season well. Serve hot with lemon wedges to squeeze over.

PER SERVING 323 kcals, protein 20g, carbs 56g, fat 4g, sat fat 2g, fibre 3g, sugar 3g, salt 3.1g

Zesty noodle stir-fry

This really packs in the vegetables towards your 5-a-day.

🕐 40 minutes   ◔ 4 (easily halved)

- 140g/5oz flat rice noodles
- 6 tbsp light soy sauce
- 5 tbsp orange juice
- ½ tsp finely grated orange zest
- 1 tsp sugar
- ½ tsp cornflour
- 1 tbsp sunflower or rapeseed oil
- ½ tbsp grated ginger
- 2 garlic cloves, finely chopped
- 2 tbsp dry sherry
- 2 red peppers, deseeded and sliced
- 2 carrots, peeled, cut into fine strips
- 2 courgettes, cut into fine strips
- 100g/4oz mangetout, sliced
- 220g can water chestnuts, sliced
- 1 bunch spring onions, shredded

1 Put the noodles in a large bowl, cover with boiling water for 4 minutes, then drain and rinse under cold water.
2 Mix the soy sauce, orange juice and zest, sugar and cornflour in a small bowl. Heat the oil in a wok, add the ginger and garlic, and fry for 1 minute. Add the sherry and peppers and fry for 1 minute. Add the carrots, courgettes and mangetout, and fry for 3 minutes. Stir in the water chestnuts and spring onions, and fry for 1 minute.
3 Add the soy-sauce mix and noodles, and stir-fry until hot. Serve straightaway.

PER SERVING 240 kcals, protein 6g, carbs 47g, fat 3g, sat fat none, fibre 4g, sugar 1.6g, salt 2.77g

Chicken & broccoli noodles

With a pack of egg noodles in your storecupboard you will always have the basis of a versatile stir fry.

 20 minutes 4

- 250g packet egg noodles
- 350g/12oz broccoli florets
- 2 tbsp olive or rapeseed oil
- 2.5cm/1in piece ginger, grated
- 4 garlic cloves, finely sliced
- 2 boneless skinless chicken breasts, cut into thin strips
- 1 bunch spring onions, trimmed and cut in half horizontally, large ones cut in half again vertically
- 3 tbsp light soy sauce
- 200ml/7fl oz chicken or vegetable stock

1 Cook the noodles in a pan of salted boiling water for 5 minutes, adding the broccoli for the last 2 minutes. Drain and set aside.

2 Meanwhile, heat a wok or frying pan until very hot. Add the oil, then stir in the ginger and garlic. Cook for 30 seconds, stirring. Add the chicken strips and cook for 5 minutes, stirring often, until tinged brown. Add the spring onions and stir briefly to heat through.

3 Mix the soy sauce and stock together, and stir into the wok or pan. Add the drained noodles and broccoli, season with black pepper and toss everything together. Serve immediately.

PER SERVING 424 kcals, protein 30g, carbs 49g, fat 12g, sat fat 2g, fibre 6g, sugar 4g, salt 2.61g

Warm Thai noodle salad

Stretch two chicken breasts to feed four in this unusual salad with a tangy dressing.

 30 minutes 4

- 2 large boneless skinless chicken breasts
- 175g/6oz medium egg noodles
- 2 good handfuls greens, such as Chinese leaf, finely shredded
- 2 carrots, cut into thin strips
- 8 spring onions, finely sliced
- 1 red pepper, deseeded and finely sliced
- handful coriander leaves

FOR THE DRESSING

- 1 red chilli, deseeded and finely chopped
- 2 garlic cloves, finely chopped
- 1 tbsp finely chopped ginger
- 2 tbsp light soy sauce
- juice 1 lime
- 2 tbsp olive or rapeseed oil

1 Heat the grill to high. Put the chicken on a baking sheet and grill for 10–12 minutes without turning, until cooked through. Meanwhile, cook the noodles according to the packet instructions. Drain and rinse in cold running water to stop them sticking together.

2 Mix the vegetables in a bowl. Thinly slice the chicken and add to the bowl, along with the noodles and coriander leaves.

3 Mix the dressing ingredients together with two tablespoons of water, pour over the salad and toss well. Serve immediately.

PER SERVING 336 kcals, protein 24g, carbs 40g, fat 10g, sat fat 1g, fibre 2g, sugar 6g, salt 1.7g

Superhealthy chicken pie

Chicken pie with its creamy filling and crisp pastry is hard to resist. Here it's given a healthy makeover by using filo pastry and packing veg into the creamy low-fat sauce.

 55 minutes 4

FOR THE FILLING
- 450ml/16fl oz chicken stock, from a cube
- 100ml/3½fl oz white wine
- 2 garlic cloves, finely chopped
- 3 thyme sprigs
- 1 tarragon sprig, plus 1 tbsp chopped leaves
- 225g/8oz carrots, cut into batons
- 500g/1lb 2oz boneless skinless chicken breasts
- 225g/8oz leeks, sliced
- 2 tbsp cornflour, mixed with 2 tbsp water
- 3 tbsp crème fraîche
- 1 heaped tsp Dijon mustard
- 1 tbsp chopped parsley leaves

FOR THE TOPPING
- 70g/2¾oz filo pastry (three 39 x 30cm/15 x 12in sheets), each sheet cut into 4
- 1 tbsp rapeseed oil

1 Pour the stock and wine into a frying pan with a lid. Add the garlic, thyme, tarragon sprig and carrots, bring to the boil then simmer for 3 minutes. Add the chicken with some pepper, cover and simmer for 5 minutes. Scatter the leeks over the chicken, cover and simmer for 10 minutes. Remove from the heat and leave to cool for 15 minutes.

2 Strain the stock into a jug – you should have 500ml/18fl oz. Tip the chicken and veg into a 1.5-litre pie dish. Discard the herbs. Pour the stock back into the pan, then slowly pour in the cornflour mix. Boil, stirring, until thick. Remove from the heat. Stir in the crème fraîche, mustard, chopped tarragon and parsley.

3 Heat oven to 200C/180C fan/gas 6. Shred the chicken meat. Stir the sauce into the chicken mixture in the dish.

4 Layer the filo on top of the filling, brushing each sheet with oil. Scrunch up the filo and tuck into the dish. Cook on a baking sheet for 25 minutes until golden.

PER SERVING 320 kcals, protein 34g, carbs 22g, fat 10g, sat fat 4g, fibre 3g, sugar 7g, salt 1.37g

Cajun-spiced chicken

This spicy rub makes the chicken really tasty; it is perfect served with new potatoes or sliced and stuffed into warm tortillas with the tzatziki and salad for a change.

 20 minutes 4

- 2 tbsp plain flour
- 2 tsp Cajun seasoning
- ¼ tsp salt
- 4 boneless skinless chicken breasts, about 140g/5oz each
- 2 tbsp olive or rapeseed oil
- tzatziki, mixed salad and new potatoes, to serve

1 Mix together the flour, Cajun seasoning and salt.
2 Rub both sides of the chicken breasts with a tablespoon of the olive oil. Dust each side with the seasoned flour. Heat the remaining oil in a frying pan.
3 Fry the coated chicken for 6–7 minutes on each side until cooked golden. Serve with the tzatziki, mixed salad and new potatoes.

PER SERVING 238 kcals, protein 35g, carbs 8g, fat 8g, sat fat 1g, fibre none, sugar 0.1g, salt 0.84g

Glazed lemon-pepper chicken

This sticky marinade turns ordinary chicken breasts into something really special.
It also works well with turkey steaks.

 15 minutes, plus marinating 4

- 4 boneless skinless chicken breasts
- 4 tbsp clear honey
- finely grated zest and juice of 1 lemon
- 2 garlic cloves, crushed
- 1 tbsp Dijon mustard
- 2 tsp ground black pepper
- 750g/1lb 10oz baby salad potatoes or larger ones, halved
- steamed broccoli florets, to serve

1 Slash each chicken breast two or three times with a sharp knife. In a shallow dish mix the honey, lemon zest and juice, garlic, mustard and black pepper for the marinade.
2 Add the chicken to the marinade and turn to coat. Leave to marinate for 30 minutes or preferably overnight.
3 Heat oven to 220C/200C fan/gas 7. Arrange the potatoes and chicken in a single layer in a shallow-sided roasting tin and pour any excess marinade on top. Roast until the potatoes are tender and the chicken is cooked, about 25-30 minutes. Serve with the steamed broccoli and any pan juices.

PER SERVING 339 kcals, protein 38g, carbs 44g, fat 3g, sat fat 1g, fibre 2g, sugar 11g, salt 0.55g

Mustard-griddled chicken, beetroot & orange salad

The combination of mustard, beetroot and orange adds a fresh and zingy flavour to this colourful salad - great for a quick supper or healthy lunch with friends.

 30 minutes 4

- 4 skinless chicken thigh fillets, sliced into thick strips
- 2 oranges
- 2 tbsp Dijon mustard
- 1 tbsp olive or rapeseed oil
- 140g bag spinach, rocket and watercress salad
- 4 vacuum-packed cooked beetroot, cut into wedges

1 Put the chicken between two sheets of baking parchment or cling film and bash with a rolling pin to flatten. Grate the zest from ½ of an orange and mix in a bowl with the mustard, 2 teaspoons of the oil and plenty of seasoning. Add the chicken and stir well.

2 Heat a griddle or frying pan and cook the chicken for 5–6 minutes on each side until cooked through. Put on a plate to rest while you assemble the salad.

3 Tip the salad leaves into a bowl. Peel and slice the oranges on a plate to catch any juices. Pour the orange juice over the leaves, add the orange slices with the remaining teaspoon of oil and toss together. Add the beetroot, then slice the chicken and add to the salad along with any resting juices. Divide everything among four plates and serve.

PER SERVING 205 kcals, protein 24g, carbs 14g, fat 6g, sat fat 1g, fibre 3g, sugar 13g, salt 1.09g

Chicken with apples & cider

This simple recipe uses only six ingredients. It also works well with pork steaks.

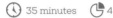 35 minutes 4

- 1–2 tbsp olive or rapeseed oil
- 4 boneless skinless chicken breasts
- 1 onion, cut into wedges
- 2 eating apples, such as Cox's, peeled, cored and each cut into 8 wedges
- 300ml/½ pint dry cider
- 150ml/¼ pint chicken stock
- rice or mashed potato, to serve

1 Heat the oil in a large frying pan with a lid and fry the chicken breasts for 3–4 minutes on each side until golden. Remove the chicken from the pan and set aside. Lower the heat slightly and add the onion. Fry, stirring, for 2–3 minutes until tinged brown. Add the apple and cook over a high heat for 5 minutes until golden.

2 Still over a high heat, pour in the cider and bubble for 2 minutes to reduce slightly. Add the stock, stirring to scrape the bits from the bottom of the pan. Lower the heat.

3 Return the chicken to the pan, cover and simmer for 5 minutes until it is almost cooked. Remove lid and simmer for 3–4 minutes to thicken the sauce a little. Season and serve with rice or mashed potato.

PER SERVING 269 kcals, protein 34g, carbs 12g, fat 7g, sat fat 1g, fibre 2g, sugar 9g, salt 0.36g

Thai-spiced chicken

· · · · · · · · · · · · · · · · · · · ·

Here's an oriental twist on a tikka marinade that, instead of curry powder, uses Thai red curry paste and chopped coriander.

 55 minutes, plus marinating 4

- 8 skinless chicken thighs
- 350g/12oz low-fat natural yogurt
- 2–3 tbsp Thai red curry paste
- 4 tbsp chopped coriander leaves
- 7.5cm/3in piece cucumber
- lime wedges, to garnish
- salad leaves, to serve

1 Heat oven to 200C/180C fan/gas 6. Put the chicken in a shallow dish in one layer. Blend a third of the yogurt, the curry paste and 3 tablespoons of the coriander. Season and pour over the chicken, turning the pieces until they are evenly coated. Leave for at least 10 minutes, or in the fridge overnight.

2 Lift the chicken on to a rack in a roasting tin and roast for 35–40 minutes, until golden. (To cook the chicken on the barbecue, reduce the cooking time to 25–30 minutes.)

3 Blend together the remaining yogurt and coriander. Finely chop the cucumber and stir into the yogurt mixture in a small bowl. Season. Serve the chicken with the yogurt dip, lime wedges and salad leaves.

· · · · · · · · · · · · · · · · · · · ·
PER SERVING 266 kcals, protein 43g, carbs 8g, fat 7g, sat fat 2g, fibre trace, sugar 6g, salt 0.69g

Chicken skewers with cucumber dip

Serve these mildly flavoured tasty skewers with Thai fragrant rice and pak choi stir-fried in a little oil.

 30 minutes 4

- 500g/1lb 2oz boneless skinless chicken breasts
- 4 tbsp chopped coriander
- juice 2 limes
- 1 tsp light muscovado sugar
- 2 garlic cloves, crushed
- 1 tbsp vegetable or rapeseed oil
- Thai fragrant rice and pak choi, to serve

FOR THE DIP
- 125ml/4fl oz rice vinegar
- 2 tbsp caster sugar
- 1 red chilli, deseeded and finely chopped
- 1 shallot, thinly sliced
- 1 cucumber

1 Cut the chicken into thin slices. Mix the coriander, 1 tablespoon of coarsely ground pepper, the lime juice, sugar, garlic and oil. Toss the chicken in this mixture, then thread on to 12 pre-soaked bamboo skewers. (You can make these up to a day ahead and chill until ready to cook.)

2 Make the dip. Heat the vinegar and sugar in a small pan until the sugar has dissolved, then increase the heat and boil for 3 minutes, until slightly syrupy. Remove from the heat and stir in the chilli and shallot. Leave to cool.

3 Quarter a 5cm/2in piece of the cucumber, then thinly slice and add to the dip. Cut the rest of the cucumber into long sticks.

4 Heat grill to high. Cook the chicken for 3–4 minutes each side, then serve with the dipping sauce, cucumber sticks, fragrant rice and pak choi.

Chicken with tomatoes & coriander

This meal in a pan comes complete with potatoes. If you did want to serve some greens too, try wilting in some spinach leaves.

 40 minutes 4

- 25g/1oz butter or 2 tbsp olive or rapeseed oil
- 4 boneless skinless chicken breasts, cut into bite-sized pieces
- 450g/1lb baby new potatoes
- 2 tsp ground coriander
- 2 tsp ground cumin
- 300ml/½ pint hot chicken stock
- 750g/1lb 10oz ripe tomatoes, cut into quarters
- splash Tabasco sauce
- squeeze lemon juice
- handful chopped coriander leaves

1 Heat the butter or oil in a large, deep-sided frying pan with a lid. Add the chicken pieces and potatoes, and stir over a medium heat for 5–7 minutes until the chicken browns. Add the spices and cook for 1 minute.

2 Pour in the stock and cook, covered, for 10 minutes until the potatoes are just tender. Remove the lid for the last 3 minutes of cooking. Add the tomatoes and cook over a medium heat, stirring occasionally, for 5 minutes until the tomatoes are hot and slightly softened.

3 Season and add a good splash of Tabasco. Squeeze over a little lemon juice and sprinkle with coriander. Serve hot.

PER SERVING 325 kcals, protein 38g, carbs 26g, fat 8g, sat fat 4g, fibre 3g, sugar 7g, salt 0.71g

Chinese chicken with pineapple

A colourful stir fry, combing sweet pineapple with vegetables for a lovely contrast of flavours and textures.

 25 minutes 4

- 1 tbsp vegetable or rapeseed oil
- 1 garlic clove, finely chopped
- 4 boneless skinless chicken breasts, cut into bite-sized pieces
- 227g can pineapple chunks in natural juice
- 2 carrots, cut into thin sticks
- 1 tbsp cornflour
- juice 1 lemon
- 2 tbsp tomato purée
- 3 tbsp light soy sauce
- 1 bunch spring onions, trimmed and cut into lengths
- rice or noodles, to serve

1 Heat the oil in a wok or frying pan. Add the garlic, stir briefly, then add the chicken. Cook, stirring, for 10 minutes.

2 Drain the pineapple chunks (save the juice). Add them to the pan with the carrots. Cook, stirring, for 2–3 minutes.

3 Add water to the reserved pineapple juice to make 200ml/7fl oz. Mix the cornflour with the lemon juice, then stir in the purée, soy sauce and diluted pineapple juice. Pour over the chicken and add the spring onions. Cook for 2 minutes more, stirring. Serve immediately with rice or noodles.

PER SERVING 277 kcals, protein 38g, carbs 19g, fat 5g, sat fat 1g, fibre 3g, sugar 12g, salt 2.4g

Chicken & broccoli stir fry

Adding a good splash of soy as the chicken cooks helps it go an even brown colour, and boosts the flavour. You could use reduced-salt soy, if you like.

 30 minutes 4

- 2 tbsp vegetable or rapeseed oil
- 450g/1lb boneless skinless chicken breasts, cut into thin strips
- 3 tbsp dark soy sauce
- 350g/12oz broccoli, broken into small florets
- 225g/8oz green beans, halved
- 1 bunch spring onions, cut into long slices
- 2 tsp cornflour
- juice 2 oranges
- 25g/1oz basil leaves, roughly torn
- rice or noodles, to serve

1 Heat the oil in a wok or large frying pan. Add the chicken strips and a splash of the soy sauce, and cook for 5 minutes, stirring, until the chicken starts to brown.
2 Stir in the broccoli, beans and half the spring onions, and cook for 3 minutes until just cooked.
3 Mix the cornflour with the orange juice and remaining soy sauce. Pour into the wok or pan and cook for about 1 minute, stirring, until just thickened. Scatter in the basil and remaining spring onions. Serve with rice or noodles.

PER SERVING 273 kcals, protein 40g, carbs 11g, fat 8g, sat fat 4g, fibre 4g, sugar 6g, salt 2.4g

Harissa chicken with chickpea salad

Harissa gives a spicy aromatic flavour to the chicken, which can be cooked on a griddle or the barbecue. This tasty salad provides three of your 5-a-day.

 25 minutes 2

- 250g punnet cherry tomatoes, halved
- ½ small red onion, chopped
- 400g can chickpeas, drained and rinsed
- small bunch parsley, roughly chopped
- juice 1 lemon
- 2 boneless skinless chicken breasts, halved lengthways through the middle
- 1 tbsp harissa paste
- fat-free natural yogurt and warmed wholemeal pitta bread, to serve

1 Mix the tomatoes, onion and chickpeas together for the salad. Stir through the parsley and lemon juice, and season. Set aside.

2 Coat the chicken with the harissa. Heat a griddle or frying pan or the barbecue. Cook the chicken for 3–4 minutes on each side until lightly charred and cooked through.

3 Divide the salad between two plates, top with the harissa chicken and serve with a dollop of yogurt and warmed pitta bread.

PER SERVING 313 kcals, protein 44g, carbs 25g, fat 5g, sat fat 1g, fibre 7g, sugar 6g, salt 1.06g

Barbecue turkey strips

This warm turkey salad is easily doubled for a crowd. Try it in wraps too.

 35 minutes, plus marinating 4

- 2 tbsp dark muscovado sugar
- 4 tbsp clear honey
- 4 tbsp light soy sauce
- 450g/1lb turkey strips
- 2 tbsp each olive oil and lemon juice
- 2 tsp caster sugar
- 1 cos lettuce, torn into pieces
- 2 large carrots, cut into sticks
- 100g/4oz beansprouts

1 Mix the muscovado sugar, half the honey and half the soy sauce in a shallow dish. Add the turkey strips and stir to coat. Cover and leave to marinate for 30 minutes.

2 Heat grill to high. Thread the turkey on to eight skewers (soak wooden ones for 20 minutes before using to prevent them burning). Grill the turkey (or barbecue) for 6 minutes each side.

3 Whisk the remaining honey and soy sauce with the olive oil, lemon juice and caster sugar. Season and toss with the lettuce and vegetables. Pile on to four plates and put the turkey on top. Serve immediately.

PER SERVING 318 kcals, protein 29g, carbs 37g, fat 7g, sat fat 1g, fibre 2g, sugar 29g, salt 2.91g

Sweet-&-sour turkey

Keep the heat high while cooking the turkey so it sizzles to a good brown colour.

 20–25 minutes 4

- 1 tbsp vegetable or rapeseed oil
- 300g/10oz turkey strips, cut into smaller strips if necessary
- 2 x 200g packs mixed baby carrots, sweetcorn and mangetout
- 1 red pepper, deseeded and sliced
- 225g/8oz beansprouts
- finely grated zest and juice 1 small orange
- 3 tbsp light soy sauce
- 1 tsp clear honey
- 2 tsp cornflour
- 2 garlic cloves, finely chopped
- cooked rice or noodles, to serve

1 Heat the oil in a wok or frying pan and fry the turkey for 3 minutes, stirring, until browned.
2 Add the baby vegetables and pepper, and fry for 4 minutes. Stir in the beansprouts.
3 Mix the orange zest and juice, soy sauce, honey, cornflour and garlic together. Pour over the stir fry and let it bubble, stirring. When the sauce has thickened, serve with rice or noodles.

PER SERVING 411 kcals, protein 24g, carbs 68g, fat 7g, sat fat 1g, fibre 4g, sugar 3g, salt 1.87g

Turkey Bolognese

· ·

We've substituted turkey mince for beef to make a low-fat version of Bolognese. You can do this for all your favourite mince recipes including lasagne and chilli too.

 40 minutes 4

- 2 tbsp olive or rapeseed oil
- 1 large onion, chopped
- 2 garlic cloves, finely chopped
- 500g/1lb 2oz minced turkey
- 400g can chopped tomatoes
- 2 tbsp tomato purée
- 300ml/½ pint chicken or beef stock
- 350g/12oz spaghetti
- 1 large courgette, finely chopped
- 6 tomatoes, deseeded and chopped
- small handful chopped flat-leaf parsley leaves, to serve

1 Heat the oil in a large pan and fry the onion and garlic for 4–5 minutes over a low heat until softened. Stir in the turkey mince and cook for 5 minutes, stirring frequently. Stir in the chopped tomatoes, tomato purée and stock. Bring to the boil then simmer, uncovered, for 10 minutes.

2 Meanwhile, cook the spaghetti according to the pack instructions. Stir the courgette and fresh tomatoes into the sauce and simmer for 5–6 minutes. Season.

3 Drain the pasta and divide among four plates. Spoon over the sauce and serve, scattered with parsley.

· ·
PER SERVING 546 kcals, protein 43g, carbs 76g, fat 10g, sat fat 2g, fibre 6g, sugar none, salt 0.75g

New potato & mince curry

Lean turkey mince replacing the more usual lamb gives a lower-fat and lighter-tasting curry.

 1 hour 4

- 450g/1lb minced turkey
- 1 tbsp vegetable or rapeseed oil
- 1 small onion, chopped
- 3 garlic cloves, finely chopped
- 1 tbsp coarsely grated ginger
- 1 red chilli, deseeded and finely sliced
- 2 tsp each ground cumin and coriander
- 1 tbsp korma curry paste
- 500g/1lb 2oz new potatoes, halved
- 100g/4oz spinach leaves
- 150g/5oz 0% fat Greek yogurt
- chapattis or naan bread, to serve

1 Heat a frying pan and dry-fry the mince. Brown it all over, stirring to break it up. Remove from the pan to a plate. Add the oil and onion to the pan, and cook for 5 minutes.

2 Stir in the garlic, ginger, chilli, spices and curry paste. Stir-fry for 1 minute. Add the mince, potatoes and 600ml/1 pint water, bring to the boil, cover, then simmer for 30 minutes. Season with salt to taste.

3 Stir in the spinach and simmer for 1 minute, uncovered, until wilted. Swirl through the yogurt and serve with Indian bread.

PER SERVING 315 kcals, protein 32g, carbs 25g, fat 10g, sat fat 3g, fibre 2g, sugar 4g, salt 0.55g

Beef & salsa burgers

Adding extra veg to a simple burger mix keeps the meat really juicy in the middle, while also boosting your 5-a-day and making it a surprisingly low-fat option too.

 20 minutes 4

- 300g/10oz lean minced beef
- 50g/2oz wholemeal breadcrumbs
- 50g/2oz carrot, grated
- 1 small onion, grated
- small handful chopped parsley leaves
- 1 tsp Worcestershire sauce
- 4 wholemeal burger buns
- handful salad leaves
- dollops tomato salsa

1 Heat grill to medium. In a large bowl, mix together the first six ingredients, then season well. Shape the mixture into four burgers and put on a baking sheet.

2 Grill the burgers for 3–4 minutes on each side until cooked through, then keep them warm. Split each burger bun in half and put under the grill, cut-side up, and lightly toast for 1 minute. Scatter some salad leaves over each toasted bun base, top with a burger, a good dollop of tomato salsa and the remaining bun half.

PER SERVING 313 kcals, protein 24g, carbs 35g, fat 10g, sat fat 4g, fibre 3g, sugar 5g, salt 1.99g

Beef tabbouleh

This speedy beef salad is a great way to use up cooked meat. Alternatively you can buy ready-cooked beef from the deli counter in any supermarket.

 35 minutes 2

- 100g/4oz bulghar wheat
- 6 slices lean rare-cooked beef
- 2–3 mint sprigs
- handful coriander
- handful cherry tomatoes
- juice 1–2 limes
- splash Thai fish sauce

1 Tip the bulghar wheat into a bowl and pour over hot water to cover. Leave, covered tightly with cling film, to absorb the liquid for 30 minutes until the grains are tender but still have bite.

2 Meanwhile, shred the beef. Then strip the leaves from the mint sprigs, chop the coriander and halve the tomatoes.

3 To serve, drain the bulghar wheat well and tip into a bowl. Tear in the mint leaves and toss with the beef, coriander, tomatoes, lime juice, fish sauce and some seasoning to taste.

PER SERVING 440 kcals, protein 54g, carbs 39g, fat 9g, sat fat 3g, fibre 0.3g, sugar 1g, salt 0.56g

Lamb steaks with barbecue sauce

· ·

Try this sauce on burgers and with lean beef and chicken too.

 25 minutes   4

- 4 lamb leg steaks, all excess fat removed
- 1 tbsp sunflower or rapeseed oil, plus a little extra for brushing
- 1 onion, chopped
- 150ml/¼ pint tomato ketchup
- 3 tbsp Worcestershire sauce
- 2 tbsp light muscovado sugar
- 2 tbsp red wine vinegar
- herby green salad, to serve

1 Season the steaks on both sides and brush with a little oil.

2 To make the sauce, heat the remaining tablespoon of the oil in a small pan, then add the onion and fry for 10 minutes until soft and lightly browned. Add the remaining ingredients, simmer gently, and stir for 5 minutes more until everything has combined into one sauce.

3 Barbecue, griddle or grill the steaks for 3–4 minutes on each side, or until cooked to your liking, and serve with the sauce on the side and a herby green salad.

· ·

PER SERVING 358 kcals, protein 34g, carbs 25g, fat 12g, sat fat 4g, fibre 1g, sugar 23g, salt 2.1g

Beef with apricots

. . . .

This rich, fruity casserole is perfect served with our butter-free, fluffy celeriac-and-potato mash.

 1½ hours   4

- 400g/14oz extra-lean stewing beef, cut into cubes
- ½ tbsp olive or rapeseed oil
- 2 large onions, chopped
- 4 garlic cloves, crushed
- 100g/4oz dried apricots, halved
- 50g/2oz sun-dried tomato halves (not in oil), roughly chopped
- 400g can chopped tomatoes

FOR THE MASH

- 450g/1lb floury potatoes, peeled and cut into small chunks
- 1 small celeriac, about 650g/1lb 7oz, peeled and cut into small chunks
- 100ml/3½fl oz skimmed milk
- grating nutmeg

1 In a non-stick pan, dry-fry the beef in two batches on a high heat until browned. Season, then remove to a plate.

2 Add the oil to the pan and fry the onions and garlic on a low heat for 4 minutes (add water if they stick). Return the beef to the pan. Add the apricots, sun-dried tomatoes, chopped tomatoes and 600ml/1 pint water, then bring to the boil, and simmer for 1 hour, stirring occasionally.

3 About 25 minutes before the end of the beef's cooking time, boil the potatoes and celeriac in a separate pan. Drain, add the milk and mash until smooth. Add the nutmeg, season to taste and serve the mash with the beef.

. . . .

PER SERVING 360 kcals, protein 31g, carbs 47g, fat 7g, sat fat 2g, fibre 12g, sugar 22g, salt 0.98g

Springtime lamb stew

An easy one-pot meal. Be sure to choose lean lamb, trimmed of fat.

 1 hour 10 minutes 4

- 2 tsp olive or rapeseed oil
- 12 shallots, peeled
- 350g/12oz trimmed diced lamb, from the chump or loin fillet
- 350g/12oz new potatoes, scrubbed and cut into chunks
- 12 baby carrots, trimmed and peeled
- 150ml/¼ pint white wine
- 250ml/9fl oz vegetable stock
- 3 bay leaves
- 200g can chopped tomatoes
- 100g/4oz frozen peas
- 1 tbsp chopped parsley leaves
- crusty bread, to serve

1 Heat the oil in a large pan and add the shallots and lamb. Fry over a medium heat until they are starting to brown, about 8–10 minutes.
2 Add the potatoes, carrots, white wine, stock, bay leaves and tomatoes to the pan. Season and bring to the boil. Cover the pan and leave the stew to simmer gently over a medium heat for 25–30 minutes until the vegetables and lamb are tender.
3 Stir in the peas and cook for another 2–3 minutes until tender. Scatter in the parsley, adjust the seasoning and serve with crusty bread, if you like.

PER SERVING 312 kcals, protein 21g, carbs 24g, fat 12g, sat fat 4g, fibre 6g, sugar 8g, salt 0.58g

Pork with pine kernels

This is a very adaptable recipe, impressive enough to cook if you have friends visiting and you are short of time.

 25 minutes 4

- 500g/1lb 2oz pork fillet, trimmed of any fat
- seasoned plain flour, for coating
- good handful flat-leaf parsley leaves, coarsely chopped
- 2 tbsp olive or rapeseed oil
- 25g/1oz pine kernels
- grated zest ½ and juice 1 lemon
- 1 tbsp clear honey
- pappardelle or tagliatelle and salad leaves, to serve

1 Cut the pork into 2cm/¾in thick slices. Toss in seasoned flour to coat very lightly and shake off excess. Heat 1 tablespoon of the oil in a large frying pan, add the pork in a single layer and fry for 3 minutes on each side, or until browned. Remove to a plate and keep warm.

2 Add the remaining tablespoon of the oil to the pan, add the pine kernels and fry until lightly browned, then stir in the lemon zest, juice and honey. Bubble briefly, stirring to make a sauce.

3 Return the pork to the pan and scatter with the parsley. Cook for 3 minutes, turning the pork, until thoroughly reheated. Serve with pappardelle or tagliatelle and some salad leaves.

PER SERVING 212 kcals, protein 28g, carbs 4g, fat 9g, sat fat 2g, fibre none, sugar 4g, salt 0.2g

Spicy pork & aubergine

Pork fillet is low in fat, and it cooks quickly, making it great for midweek meals. Here it's used in a mild curry.

 35 minutes 4

- 1 tbsp olive or rapeseed oil
- 2 onions, sliced
- 1 small aubergine, trimmed and diced
- 500g/1lb 2oz lean pork fillet, trimmed of any fat and sliced
- 2 red peppers, deseeded and cut into chunky strips
- 2–3 tbsp mild curry powder
- 400g can plum tomatoes
- basmati rice, to serve

1 Heat the oil in a large non-stick frying pan with a lid. Tip in the onions and aubergine, and fry for 8 minutes, stirring frequently, until soft and golden brown.

2 Tip in the pork and fry for 5 minutes, stirring occasionally, until it starts to brown. Mix in the pepper strips and stir-fry for about 3 minutes until soft.

3 Sprinkle in the curry powder. Stir-fry for a minute, then pour in the tomatoes and 150ml/¼ pint water. Stir vigorously, cover the pan and leave the curry to simmer for 5 minutes until the tomatoes break down to form a thick sauce (you can add a drop more water, if the mixture gets too thick). Season and serve with basmati rice.

PER SERVING 293 kcals, protein 31g, carbs 16g, fat 11g, sat fat 2g, fibre 6g, sugar 13g, salt 0.4g

Tandoori-lamb skewers with crunchy slaw & raita

• •

This fantastic – and colourful – recipe contains two of your 5-a-day fruit-and-veg portions, so it makes a great healthy supper. It's easily doubled or trebled.

 20 minutes   2

- 1 tbsp tandoori paste
- 4 tbsp 0% fat Greek yogurt
- 175g/6oz leg of lamb steak, all visible fat removed, cubed
- small bunch coriander leaves, chopped
- wholemeal chapattis, to serve

FOR THE SLAW
- 1 carrot, peeled and sliced into strips with a peeler
- ¼ white cabbage, shredded
- 1 red onion, sliced
- juice 1 lime
- 2 tsp olive or rapeseed oil
- 1 tsp mustard seeds

1 In a medium bowl, combine the tandoori paste with 2 tablespoons of the yogurt. Add the lamb, mixing to coat all the pieces.

2 Make the raita by mixing the remaining yogurt with 1 tablespoon of the chopped coriander and some seasoning, then set aside. For the slaw, mix together all of the vegetables and the remaining coriander in a large bowl, then stir in the lime juice, oil and mustard seeds.

3 Heat grill to high. Divide the lamb among four skewers, grill for 3–4 minutes on each side, until lightly charred and cooked through. Serve with the slaw, raita and warmed chapattis.

• •

PER SERVING 270 kcals, protein 25g, carbs 17g, fat 10g, sat fat 2g, fibre 6g, sugar 14g, salt 0.5g

Toad-in-the-hole

A low-fat version of an old favourite. Be sure to choose the sausages carefully, by checking their fat content on the packet.

 1 hour 20 minutes   4

- 1 red onion, cut into wedges, layers separated
- 8 thick low-fat pork sausages
- 1 tsp olive or rapeseed oil
- steamed carrots and cabbage, to serve

FOR THE BATTER
- 100g/4oz plain flour
- 1 medium egg
- 300ml/½ pint skimmed milk
- 2 tsp wholegrain mustard
- 1 tsp thyme leaves

1 Heat oven to 200C/180C fan/gas 6. Tip the onions into a small shallow non-stick roasting tin (about 23 x 30cm). Arrange the sausages on top of the onions, then add the oil and roast for 20 minutes.

2 While the sausages are roasting, make the batter. Sift the flour into a bowl, drop the egg in the centre and beat in the milk a little at a time until it makes a smooth batter. Stir in the mustard and thyme, and season.

3 Pour the batter quickly into the tin and return to the oven for 40 minutes, until the batter is risen and golden. Serve with steamed carrots and cabbage.

PER SERVING 293 kcals, protein 23g, carbs 36g, fat 7g, sat fat 2g, fibre 1g, sugar 7g, salt 2.36g

Ham & vegetable casserole

A simple dish packed with healthy vegetables. You could use gammon, but make sure it is lean.

 45 minutes  4

- 1 tbsp olive oil
- 1 large onion, chopped
- 500g/1lb 2oz waxy new potatoes, halved
- 1 red pepper, deseeded and cut into chunks
- 500g/1lb 2oz ripe tomatoes, quartered
- 150ml/¼ pint vegetable or chicken stock
- 1 tsp dried or 1 tbsp chopped thyme leaves
- 3 courgettes, about 375g/13oz total, thickly sliced
- 175g/6oz slice thick ham, cut into strips
- handful chopped parsley leaves

1 Heat the oil in a large pan. Add the onion and cook, stirring often, for 8 minutes or until golden. Tip in the potatoes, pepper, tomatoes, stock and thyme. Season well.

2 Cover, bring to the boil and simmer and cook for 25 minutes, stirring from time to time until the potatoes are almost tender and the tomatoes have begun to break down to form a sauce.

3 Add the courgettes and simmer for 5 minutes. Stir in the ham and parsley, and heat through. Season and serve.

PER SERVING 272 kcals, protein 16g, carbs 34g, fat 9g, sat fat 2g, fibre 5g, sugar 12g, salt 1.35g

Ham, leek & Camembert grill

· ·

If you don't have Camembert, use crumbled Stilton or mature reduced-fat Cheddar instead.

 25 minutes 4

- 600ml/1 pint chicken or vegetable stock
- 700g/1lb 9oz scrubbed unpeeled potatoes, thickly sliced
- 450g/1lb leeks, sliced
- 100g/4oz wafer-thin ham
- 125g packet Camembert, thinly sliced

1 In a large pan, heat the stock to boiling, then add the potatoes. Cook for 15 minutes until just tender, adding the leeks for the last 5 minutes of cooking time. Drain, reserving 4 tablespoons of the stock.

2 Heat the grill to high. Layer up the sliced potatoes and leeks with the ham in a shallow heatproof dish and season between the layers.

3 Pour over the reserved stock. Lay the cheese on top, then grill for 5 minutes until the cheese has melted and is beginning to brown. Serve immediately.

· ·

PER SERVING 280 kcals, protein 17g, carbs 34g, fat 9g, sat fat 5g, fibre 5g, sugar 4g, salt 1.81g

Fish, chips & mushy peas

This takeaway classic can easily be made healthy yet remain as delicious as the original. This tasty low-fat version is high in fibre, folic acid and vitamin C.

 50 minutes 2

- 400g/14oz baking potatoes
- 2 tsp olive or rapeseed oil
- 2 slices white bread
- 2 white fish fillets
- 1 tbsp plain flour, seasoned
- 1 egg, beaten
- 140g/5oz frozen peas with mint
- 2 tbsp half-fat crème fraîche

1 Heat oven to 200C/180C fan/gas 6. Peel the potatoes, cut into thick chips, then toss with the oil and a little salt. Arrange them on a large non-stick baking sheet and roast for 20 minutes, turning halfway through.

2 Lightly toast the bread, then pulse briefly in a food processor to make coarse breadcrumbs. Dust the fish in the flour, shaking off the excess, then dip it first into the egg and then the breadcrumbs, and coat thoroughly. Roast the fish with the chips for a further 20 minutes or until both are golden.

3 Just before the fish and chips are ready, boil the peas for 3–4 minutes, then drain and mash. Stir in the crème fraîche and season, then serve with the fish and chips.

PER SERVING 484 kcals, protein 42g, carbs 58g, fat 11g, sat fat 3g, fibre 6g, sugar 4g, salt 1.09g

Spiced cod with crispy onions

Cod cooks very quickly so time it carefully – just a few minutes too long can make the flesh tough and dry.

 25 minutes, plus marinating   4

- 4 cod fillets, about 140g/5oz each
- 200g tub Greek yogurt
- 1 tbsp tikka masala paste
- 2 tbsp chopped ginger
- juice ½ lemon
- 225g/8oz long grain rice
- 140g/5oz green beans, halved
- 1 tbsp vegetable or rapeseed oil
- 1 small onion, finely sliced

1 Put the fish in a single layer in a shallow heatproof dish. Mix together the yogurt, curry paste, half the ginger and the lemon juice to make a marinade. Season. Pour the marinade over the fish, turning to coat. Set aside to marinate for 30 minutes.

2 Heat grill to high. Cook the rice in boiling water for 12–15 minutes, adding the beans for the last 4 minutes. Grill the fish in its marinade for 8–10 minutes, until the cod is cooked.

3 Meanwhile, heat the oil in a pan. Fry the onion and remaining ginger for 8 minutes over a medium heat until golden and crisp. Drain on kitchen paper. Drain the rice and beans well. Serve the fish with the marinade, rice and green beans. Top with the gingery fried onions.

PER SERVING 408 kcals, protein 34g, carbs 49g, fat 10g, sat fat 3g, fibre 1g, sugar 4g, salt 0.46g

Cod with lemon & parsley

Shallow-fried fish needs a light dusting of flour to protect it from the fierce heat, and the flour makes a tasty, golden crust.

 20 minutes   2

- 2 cod fillets, about 175g/6oz each
- 2 tbsp plain flour, seasoned
- 25g/1oz butter
- juice 1 lemon
- 1 heaped tbsp chopped parsley leaves
- new potatoes and greens or runner beans, to serve

1 Coat the cod fillets with the flour, dusting off any excess.
2 Heat half the butter in a frying pan. When it is bubbling, add the fish, skin-side down, and cook over a fairly high heat for about 4–5 minutes. Using a fish slice, turn the fillets carefully and brown the other side. When the fish is just cooked (the flesh will start to flake and become opaque), add the remaining butter to the pan. When it is bubbling, stir in the lemon juice and season.
3 Bubble the sauce up until it is slightly thickened, then stir in the parsley. Serve with new potatoes and greens or runner beans.

PER SERVING 304 kcals, protein 34g, carbs 15g, fat 12g, sat fat 7g, fibre 1g, sugar 1g, salt 0.77g

Mediterranean cod

Mixed-pepper antipasto is available in jars in most supermarkets and delicatessens.

 1 hour 4

- 750g/1lb 10oz floury potatoes, cut into wedges
- 2 tbsp olive or rapeseed oil
- 4 cod fillets, about 140g/5oz each
- 225g/8oz chestnut mushrooms
- 8 tbsp mixed-pepper antipasto
- 2 tbsp grated Parmesan

1 Heat oven to 200C/180C fan/gas 6. Put the potato wedges in a roasting tin. Drizzle over the oil and stir well. Season. Cook in the middle of the oven for 45–50 minutes, stirring halfway through, until the potatoes are golden, crisp and cooked through.
2 Meanwhile, put the cod fillets in an ovenproof dish in a single layer. Season well. Slice the mushrooms and scatter over the fish.
3 Spread the mixed-pepper antipasto over the top of the mushrooms. Put the fish in the oven on the shelf above the potato wedges 10 minutes before the wedges have finished cooking. Sprinkle the fish with the grated Parmesan and serve hot with the potato wedges.

PER SERVING 391 kcals, protein 35g, carbs 32g, fat 12g, sat fat 3g, fibre 5g, sugar 3g, salt 1.3g

Zesty haddock with crushed potatoes & peas

Salmon fillets could replace the haddock here – just cook the fish for an extra few minutes. As well as being low in fat, this dish is a good source of vitamin C.

 35 minutes 4

- 600g/1lb 5oz floury potatoes, unpeeled, cut into chunks
- 140g/5oz frozen peas
- 2½ tbsp extra virgin olive oil
- juice and zest ½ lemon
- 1 tbsp capers, roughly chopped
- 2 tbsp snipped chives
- 4 haddock or other chunky white fish fillets, about 120g/4½oz each
- 2 tbsp seasoned plain flour
- steamed broccoli, to serve

1 Cover the potatoes in cold water in a pan, bring to the boil, then lower to a simmer. Cook for 10 minutes until tender, adding the peas for the final minute of cooking. Drain and roughly crush together, adding plenty of seasoning and 1 tablespoon of the oil. Keep warm.

2 Meanwhile, for the dressing, mix 1 tablespoon of the oil, the lemon juice and zest, capers and chives with some seasoning.

3 Dust the fish in the flour, tapping off any excess, and season. Heat the remaining oil in a non-stick frying pan. Fry the fish for 2–3 minutes on each side until cooked, then add the dressing and warm through. Serve with the potato-and-pea crush and some steamed broccoli.

PER SERVING 305 kcals, protein 28g, carbs 31g, fat 8g, sat fat 1g, fibre 4g, sugar 2g, salt 0.71g

Smoked-haddock fishcakes

Cooked peas add extra colour and flavour to these simple fishcakes.

 50 minutes   3

- 450g/1lb peeled potatoes, cut into chunks
- 2 eggs
- 225g/8oz skinless smoked haddock fillets
- 4 tbsp skimmed milk
- knob butter
- 175g/6oz frozen peas, cooked
- 100g/4oz white breadcrumbs
- 1 tbsp vegetable oil
- salad leaves, to serve

1 Heat oven to 200C/180C fan/gas 6. Boil the potatoes and eggs in salted water for 10–12 minutes. Meanwhile put the fish, milk and butter in a pan, season, cover and simmer for 4–5 minutes. Strain and reserve the liquor. Flake the fish.

2 Drain the potatoes and eggs. Shell the eggs and mash them with the potatoes. Add the liquor, season and stir in the fish and peas. Shape into six cakes. Press into the breadcrumbs, coating evenly.

3 Pour the oil into a roasting tin. Heat for 5 minutes in the oven. Add the fishcakes, coat in the oil and cook for 25–30 minutes, turning halfway through. Serve with salad leaves.

PER SERVING 442 kcals, protein 29g, carbs 55g, fat 10g, sat fat 2g, fibre 7g, sugar 4g, salt 2.3g

Soy salmon with sesame stir fry

A superhealthy and versatile fish, salmon takes on the strong flavours of Chinese cooking very well.

🕐 30 minutes, plus marinating   4

- 4 salmon fillets, about 100g/4oz each
- 3 tbsp soy sauce
- 2 tbsp clear honey
- finely grated zest and juice 1 lemon
- 2 garlic cloves, thinly sliced
- 2.5cm/1in piece ginger, finely grated
- 8 spring onions, finely shredded

FOR THE STIR-FRY
- 1 tsp sesame oil
- 100g/4oz mangetout
- 2 medium carrots, cut into matchsticks
- 100g/4oz baby corn, halved
- 2 courgettes, cut into matchsticks

1 Put the salmon in a shallow dish. Heat the soy sauce, honey, lemon zest and juice, garlic and ginger in a small pan with 1 tablespoon water for 4 minutes. Pour the soy-sauce mix over the salmon and scatter with most of the spring onions. Leave to marinate in the fridge for at least 30 minutes.

2 Heat the grill or a griddle pan. Remove the salmon, reserving the marinade. Grill or griddle the salmon for 8 minutes, turning once, until tender and golden.

3 Meanwhile, heat a wok or large frying pan to really hot and add the sesame oil. Add the mangetout, carrots and corn, and stir-fry for 2 minutes. Add the courgettes and stir-fry for 2 minutes. Add the reserved marinade and cook for 2–3 minutes. Serve with the salmon and remaining spring onion.

PER SERVING 280 kcals, protein 23g, carbs 18g, fat 12g, sat fat 2.5g, fibre 3g, sugar 13g, salt 2.6g

Lemon-fried mackerel

Heart-healthy mackerel are high in omega-3. Try to eat mackerel or other oily fish at least once a week.

 25 minutes   4

- 2 lemons
- 4 small cleaned mackerel
- 1 tbsp vegetable or rapeseed oil
- 3 tbsp light soy sauce
- 1 tsp caster sugar
- stir-fried rice or noodles, to serve

1 Thinly slice one of the lemons. Season the fish then put the lemon slices down the length of each. Tie in place with string.

2 Heat the oil in a large frying pan and cook the fish, lemon-side down, for 3–4 minutes until well browned. Turn and cook the other side for 3 minutes.

3 Add the soy sauce, 4 tablespoons water and the sugar to the pan. Squeeze in the juice of the remaining lemon and simmer for 2–3 minutes until the fish is cooked through. Serve on a bed of stir-fried rice or noodles, spooning over the pan juices.

PER SERVING 163 kcals, protein 28g, carbs 4g, fat 4g, sat fat 1g, fibre none, sugar 1.5g, salt 2.27g

Prawns with tomato & feta

Although already qualifying for low fat, you can use a reduced-fat feta in this if you want to lower the fat content even more.

 20 minutes   4

- 2 tbsp olive oil
- 2 onions, finely chopped
- 2 x 400g cans chopped tomatoes in rich tomato sauce
- pinch sugar
- 350g/12oz large cooked peeled prawns, thawed if frozen
- 100g/4oz feta
- rice or pasta, to serve
- 3 tbsp chopped parsley leaves

1 Heat the oil in a frying pan, add the onions and fry gently for about 7 minutes, until softened and light brown. Add the tomatoes and sugar, and simmer for 5 minutes.
2 Throw in the prawns, season and cook gently for 5 minutes until they are thoroughly hot.
3 Serve the prawns spooned over some rice or pasta. Crumble over the feta and sprinkle with chopped parsley.

PER SERVING 186 kcals, protein 22g, carbs 11g, fat 6g, sat fat 3g, fibre 3g, sugar 9g, salt 1.54g

Quick seafood paella

With a bag of frozen seafood in the freezer you can make this speedy version of a classic Spanish dish.

 30 minutes 4

- 1 tbsp olive or rapeseed oil
- 1 onion, finely chopped
- 1 red pepper, deseeded and sliced
- 2 garlic cloves, finely chopped
- 230g can chopped tomatoes
- 1 tsp ground turmeric
- 300g/10oz long grain rice
- 1.3 litres/2¼ pints vegetable stock
- 450g bag frozen mixed seafood (prawns, mussels and squid rings), thawed
- 175g/6oz green beans, halved
- handful chopped flat-leaf parsley leaves
- 1 lemon, cut into wedges

1 Heat the oil in a large frying pan and cook the onion and pepper for 5 minutes until softened but not brown. Stir in the garlic, tomatoes and turmeric, and cook for 1 minute more, stirring occasionally.

2 Tip in the rice and cook for 1 minute, stirring to coat the grains. Pour in the stock, stir well and bring to the boil, then simmer uncovered for 8 minutes, stirring occasionally, until the rice is almost cooked and most of the stock has been absorbed.

3 Add the seafood and beans, and cook for 3–4 minutes more. Stir in the parsley and season. Serve straight from the pan with lemon wedges.

PER SERVING 463 kcals, protein 32g, carbs 75g, fat 6g, sat fat 1g, fibre 3g, sugar 10g, salt 1.91g

Black-bean chilli

Comforting, delicious and healthy. The cumin and cider vinegar add a lovely dimension to this dish.

 40 minutes 4–6

- 2 tbsp olive or rapeseed oil
- 4 garlic cloves, finely chopped
- 2 large onions, chopped
- 3 tbsp sweet pimentón (Spanish paprika) or mild chilli powder
- 3 tbsp ground cumin
- 3 tbsp cider vinegar
- 2 tbsp brown sugar
- 2 x 400g cans chopped tomatoes
- 2 x 400g cans black beans, drained and rinsed
- boiled long grain rice plus some, or one, of the following toppings, to serve: crumbled feta, chopped spring onions, sliced radishes, avocado chunks

1 In a large pan, heat the oil and fry the garlic and onions for 5 minutes until almost softened. Add the pimentón or chilli powder and cumin, cook for a few minutes, then add the vinegar, sugar, tomatoes and some seasoning. Cook for 10 minutes.
2 Pour in the beans and cook for another 10 minutes. Serve with rice and the accompaniments of your choice in small bowls. Let people add their own topping to their chilli.

PER SERVING (4) 339 kcals, protein 17g, carbs 50g, fat 10g, sat fat 1g, fibre 8g, sugar 20g, salt 1.45g

Chargrilled peppers with couscous

Don't let eating alone be an excuse not to eat well.

 10 minutes 1

- 50g/2oz couscous
- 2 tbsp sultanas or raisins
- ½ garlic clove, finely grated
- 1 red pepper and ½ yellow or orange pepper, deseeded and quartered
- ½ lemon, cut into wedges
- 1 tsp olive oil
- 2 tbsp chopped parsley or coriander leaves

1 Put the couscous and sultanas or raisins in a bowl, with the garlic. Pour over 150ml/ ¼ pint boiling water and leave, covered, for 5 minutes until the water is absorbed. Heat grill to high.
2 Put the peppers, skin-side up, on the grill rack with the lemon wedges, brush with the oil and grill for 5 minutes until the pepper skins are blackened (leave the skins on for a smoky flavour). Stir the herbs into the couscous and season.
3 Spoon the couscous on to a plate, top with the peppers and squeeze over the juice from the grilled lemon. Serve immediately.

PER SERVING 326 kcals, protein 7g, carbs 63g, fat 7g, sat fat 1g, fibre 5g, sugar 35g, salt 0.05g

Spicy-vegetable chapatti wraps

Curry can be deceivingly high in fat – this version is packed with flavour and has only 7g fat per serving.

 25 minutes 4

- 300g/10oz sweet potatoes, peeled and roughly cubed
- 400g can peeled plum tomatoes
- 400g can chickpeas, drained and rinsed
- ½ tsp chilli flakes
- 2 tbsp mild curry paste
- 100g/4oz baby leaf spinach
- 2 tbsp chopped coriander leaves
- 4 plain chapattis
- 4 tbsp fat-free Greek yogurt

1 Cook the sweet potatoes in salted boiling water for 10–12 minutes until tender. Meanwhile, put the tomatoes, chickpeas, chilli flakes and curry paste in another pan, and simmer gently for about 5 minutes, stirring all the time.

2 Heat grill to high. Drain the sweet potatoes and add to the tomato mixture. Stir in the spinach and cook for a minute until just starting to wilt. Stir in the coriander, season to taste and keep warm.

3 Sprinkle the chapattis with a little water and grill for 20–30 seconds each side. Spoon on the vegetable filling, top with yogurt and fold in half to serve.

PER SERVING 351 kcals, protein 14g, carbs 54g, fat 7g, sat fat 1g, fibre 8g, sugar 10g, salt 1.5g

Spiced bulghar & squash salad

If 'satisfying' and 'salad' aren't two words you'd put together, this warmly spiced dish might change your mind.

 30-40 minutes 4

- 1 butternut squash, about 1kg/2lb 4oz, peeled, deseeded and cut into small chunks
- 2 red peppers, deseeded and roughly sliced
- 2 tbsp harissa paste
- 1 tbsp olive or rapeseed oil
- 140g/5oz bulghar wheat
- 600ml/1 pint hot vegetable stock
- 1 garlic clove, crushed
- juice ½ lemon
- 150g pot natural bio-yogurt
- 400g can chickpeas, drained and rinsed
- 180g bag baby leaf spinach

1 Heat oven to 200C/180C fan/gas 6. Toss the squash and red pepper in the harissa paste and oil. Spread the chunks out on a large baking sheet and roast for 20 minutes until softened and the edges of the vegetables are starting to char.

2 Meanwhile put the bulghar wheat in a large bowl and pour over the hot stock, then cover tightly with cling film and leave to absorb the liquid for 15 minutes until the grains are tender, but still have a little bite. In a separate bowl, mix the garlic and lemon juice into the yogurt and season to taste.

3 Let the bulghar wheat cool slightly then toss in the roasted vegetables, chickpeas and spinach – the leaves may wilt a little. Season, if you want, drizzle with the garlicky yogurt and serve warm.

PER SERVING 410 kcals, protein 16g, carbs 66g, fat 9g, sat fat 1g, fibre 9g, sugar 21g, salt 1.18g

Veggie rice pot

Forget the takeaway and make your own Chinese special rice at home. You can add all sorts of other veg to this too, such as beansprouts, broccoli florets and baby corn.

 35 minutes 4

- 1 tbsp sunflower or rapeseed oil
- 2 peppers (1 red, 1 yellow), deseeded and thickly sliced
- 250g pack shiitake or chestnut mushrooms, sliced
- 250g/9oz long grain rice (not the easy-cook type)
- 2 garlic cloves, finely chopped
- 1 heaped tsp five-spice powder
- 3 tbsp dry sherry
- 140g/5oz frozen petits pois
- 1 tsp sesame oil
- 2 eggs, beaten
- 1 bunch spring onions, sliced diagonally
- 1 tbsp light soy sauce, or more if you like

1 Boil the kettle. Heat the oil in a large, deep frying pan with a lid, then add the peppers and mushrooms. Fry over a high heat for 3 minutes or until starting to soften and turn golden. Turn down the heat, then stir in the rice, garlic and five-spice. Sizzle for 2 minutes, then splash in the sherry and top up with 350ml/12fl oz hot water.

2 Cover the pan and simmer for 15–20 minutes until all of the liquid has been absorbed and the rice is tender, stirring now and again. Add the peas for the final few minutes.

3 Heat another frying pan, add a drop of the sesame oil, then add the eggs. Swirl them around the pan to make a thin omelette. Once set, turn out on to a board, roll up and shred thinly. Tip the egg and spring onions on to the rice, fluff up with a fork, season with soy sauce and the remaining sesame oil, then serve.

PER SERVING 377 kcals, protein 12g, carbs 67g, fat 9g, sat fat 2g, fibre 4g, sugar 9g, salt 1.14g

Vegetable paella

A veggie version of the traditional Spanish rice dish. Smoked paprika adds extra flavour, but unsmoked paprika works too.

 35 minutes   4

- 2 tbsp olive or rapeseed oil
- 1 onion, finely chopped
- 1 garlic clove, crushed
- 1 red pepper, deseeded and finely chopped
- 1 green pepper, deseeded and finely chopped
- 100g/4oz chestnut mushrooms, sliced
- 225g/8oz long grain rice
- 850ml/1½ pints vegetable stock
- ½ tsp smoked or unsmoked paprika
- large pinch saffron strands
- 85g/3oz frozen peas
- 2 tomatoes, deseeded and finely diced
- 2 tbsp chopped flat-leaf parsley leaves
- green salad, to serve

1 Heat the oil in a frying pan and fry the onion for 2–3 minutes, stirring occasionally, until softened. Add the garlic, red and green peppers and mushrooms, and cook for a further 2–3 minutes, stirring occasionally.
2 Stir in the rice and fry for 1 minute. Stir in the stock, paprika and saffron. Bring to the boil and simmer for 10–12 minutes, stirring occasionally, until the rice is just tender (top up with more water if necessary). Stir in the peas and cook for a further 2–3 minutes. Season to taste.
3 Spoon the paella on to serving plates and sprinkle over the tomato and parsley. Serve immediately with a green salad.

PER SERVING 324 kcals, protein 7g, carbs 58g, fat 9g, sat fat 1g, fibre 4g, sugar 7g, salt 0.06g

Summery Provençal apricots

The dimpled fresh apricots look lovely left whole, but you can halve and stone them before poaching, if you prefer.

 40 minutes 4

- 175cl bottle dry fruity rosé wine
- 175g/6oz golden caster sugar
- 1 vanilla pod, split open lengthways with a sharp knife, then cut in 4 (keep the seeds inside)
- 700g/1lb 9oz ripe apricots
- vanilla ice-cream, to serve

1 Pour the wine into a pan, tip in the sugar and then add the pieces of vanilla pod. Stir over a low heat until the sugar has dissolved.

2 Add the apricots. Cover and gently poach until just softened – about 15–20 minutes for whole fruit and 10–15 minutes for halves.

3 Lift the apricots out with a slotted spoon and put them in a bowl. Boil the liquid hard for 8–10 minutes to make a thin syrup. Pour over the apricots and leave to cool. Serve warm or cold, with a piece of vanilla pod to decorate and a scoop of vanilla ice-cream.

PER SERVING 356 kcals, protein 2g, carbs 62g, fat 0.2g, sat fat none, fibre 3g, sugar 60g, salt 0.03g

Sticky cinnamon figs

A simple but stylish pudding, ready in just 10 minutes, that uses only five ingredients.

 10 minutes   4

- 8 ripe figs
- large knob butter
- 4 tbsp clear honey
- handful shelled pistachio nuts or almonds
- 1 tsp ground cinnamon or mixed spice
- low-fat crème fraîche or natural yogurt, to serve

1 Heat the grill to medium–high. Cut a deep cross in the top of each fig then ease the top apart like a flower. Sit the figs in a baking dish and drop a small piece of the butter into the centre of each fruit. Drizzle the honey over the figs, then sprinkle with the nuts and spice.

2 Grill for 5 minutes until the figs are softened and the honey and butter make a sticky sauce in the bottom of the dish. Serve warm, with dollops of low-fat crème fraîche or yogurt, if you like.

PER SERVING 162 kcals, protein 3g, carbs 23g, fat 7g, sat fat 2g, fibre 2g, sugar 11.5g, salt 0.06

Low-fat tiramisu

A classic Italian dessert reinvented.

 45 minutes, plus cooling and overnight chilling   8

- 250ml/9fl oz strong hot coffee, preferably freshly ground
- 1 tbsp golden caster sugar
- 4 tbsp Marsala wine
- 18 sponge fingers, preferably Savoiardi
- ½ tsp cocoa powder, to dust
- few raspberries, to decorate
  FOR THE FILLING
- 1 tbsp each golden caster sugar and cornflour
- 150ml/¼ pint semi-skimmed milk
- 1 medium egg, separated
- ½ vanilla pod, split lengthways
- 85g/3oz half-fat crème fraîche
- 1 tbsp Marsala
- 140g/5oz light mascarpone
- 100g/4oz light soft cheese

1 Stir the coffee, sugar and Marsala together in a shallow dish. Set aside.
2 Blend the sugar, cornflour and 1 tablespoon of the milk for the filling to a paste in a medium pan. Beat in the egg yolk, then the remaining milk. Add the vanilla and stir over a low heat for 8–10 minutes without boiling. Remove from the heat; stir in the crème fraîche and Marsala. Cover with cling film. Cool.
3 Line a 900g loaf tin with cling film. Beat together the mascarpone and soft cheese, then stir into the rest of the filling. Whisk the egg white to stiff peaks then fold this in.
4 Briefly dip one of the sponge fingers in the coffee mixture. Lay lengthways in the the tin. Do the same with 5 more, so they cover the bottom of the tin. Spread over half of the filling, then repeat with 6 more of the biscuits and the remaining filling. Dip and lay the remaining sponge fingers on top. Cover with cling film and chill overnight.
5 Turn out and peel off the cling film. Dust with cocoa and scatter with raspberries to serve.

PER SERVING 220 kcals, protein 6g, carbs 26g, fat 10g, sat fat 6g, fibre 0.3g, sugar 17g, salt 0.25g

Melon & ginger sorbet

Check the melons are really ripe and fragrant for the best flavour.

🕐 15 minutes, plus freezing   4

- 2 ripe Galia melons (about 1.5kg/3lb 5oz total), halved and deseeded
- 85g/3oz caster sugar
- 4 balls stem ginger in syrup, drained and chopped, plus extra to decorate (optional)
- 1 medium egg white

1 Scoop out the flesh from the melons and put in a food processor with the sugar. Blend until smooth, then stir in the ginger and transfer to a shallow freezerproof dish. Freeze for 2 hours until mushy.

2 Whisk the egg white until just stiff, but not dry. Remove the iced melon from the freezer and mash with a fork, then stir in the egg white.

3 Return to the freezer for a further 2 hours until frozen. Serve decorated with extra stem ginger, if liked.

PER SERVING 173 kcals, protein 3g, carbs 42g, fat 0.4g, sat fat 0.01g, fibre 2g, sugar 21g, salt 0.33g

Zesty strawberries with Cointreau

If you're also making this fat-free dessert for children, simply splash a little Cointreau over the adult portions when you serve.

 5 minutes, plus 1 hour soaking   4

- 500g/1lb 2oz strawberries, hulled and halved or quartered, depending on size
- 3 tbsp Cointreau
- zest 1 orange
- 4 tbsp icing sugar
- mint leaves, roughly torn, to scatter

1 Tip the strawberries into a large bowl. Splash over the Cointreau, add the orange zest and sift in the icing sugar, then give everything a really good mix. Cover, then leave for 1 hour or more for the juices to become syrupy and the strawberries to soak up some of the alcohol.

2 To serve, scatter the mint leaves over the strawberries and give them one more good stir, then spoon into four individual glass dishes.

PER SERVING 69 kcals, protein 1g, carbs 10g, fat none, sat fat none, fibre 1g, sugar 10g, salt 0.02g

Poached pears with blackberries

For a special occasion, substitute half the apple juice with 150ml/¼ pint red wine.

 40 minutes 4

- 4 medium pears
- zest 1 lemon (peel off with a potato peeler)
- 1 tbsp lemon juice
- 250g/9oz blackberries
- 300ml/½ pint unsweetened apple juice
- 50g/2oz golden caster sugar
- 8 tbsp 0% fat Greek yogurt

1 Peel the pears but don't remove their stalks. Put the pears in a pan with the lemon zest and juice, half the blackberries, the apple juice and caster sugar. Heat until simmering, then cover and cook gently for 20–25 minutes until the pears are tender, turning them once.

2 Remove the pears from the liquid and cool for a few minutes. Halve each, core with a teaspoon or melon baller and transfer to four dishes.

3 Strain the pear liquid through a sieve, into a pan. Add the remaining blackberries and warm gently. Serve the pears with the saucy blackberries and the yogurt.

PER SERVING 180 kcals, protein 5g, carbs 41g, fat none, sat fat none, fibre 5g, sugar 13g, salt trace

Banana & apricot compote

The apricots can be cooked up to 2 days ahead and stored in the fridge. Try serving this for a healthy breakfast too.

 30 minutes, plus cooling   4

- 250g/9oz ready-to-eat dried apricots
- 200ml/7fl oz apple juice
- 2 bananas, sliced
- 4 passion fruit (or punnet of raspberries)
- 2 tbsp toasted flaked almonds
- yogurt or crème fraîche and biscuits, to serve

1 Put the apricots, apple juice and 200ml/7fl oz water in a pan. Bring to the boil, cover and simmer for 20 minutes.

2 Remove from the heat and leave to cool – you can make ahead up to this stage.

3 Tip the cooled apricots into a bowl and stir in the banana. Mix in the flesh from the passion fruit (or the raspberries). Sprinkle the almonds over the fruit and serve with yogurt or crème fraîche, and some biscuits.

PER SERVING 259 kcals, protein 6g, carbs 43g, fat 5g, sat fat trace, fibre 8g, sugar 41g, salt 0.13g

Crunchy custard-baked apples

No need for your diet to be pudding free when these lovely baked apples are this low in fat and calories.

 50 minutes   6

- 500g carton ready-made custard (not from the chiller cabinet)
- 6 Bramley apples, halved through the middle and core removed
- zest and juice 1 orange
- 1 tsp ground cinnamon
- 1 tbsp golden caster sugar
- 6 tbsp crunchy granola with almonds
- low-fat natural yogurt or vanilla ice cream, to serve (optional)

1 Heat oven to 180C/160C fan/gas 4. Pour the custard into a large baking dish. In a large bowl, toss the apples in the orange zest and juice, cinnamon and sugar.

2 Arrange the apples, cut-side up, on top of the custard and drizzle with any extra juice from the bowl. Sprinkle over the granola and bake for 30 minutes, until the apples are soft and piping hot – cover after 20 minutes if the granola is getting dark. Serve with a spoon of low-fat yogurt or a scoop of ice cream, if you like.

PER SERVING 166 kcals, protein 4g, carbs 27g, fat 4g, sat fat none, fibre 3g, sugar 24g, salt 0.1g

Cheat's clafoutis

This is an easy, no-fuss cherry-and-lemon version of the classic French recipe.

 50 minutes   2–3

- oil, for greasing
- 450g/1lb cherries, pitted
- 2 tbsp cherry, plum or apricot jam
- finely grated zest and juice 1 lemon
- 50g/2oz plain flour
- 3 eggs
- 450ml/16fl oz skimmed milk
- ½ tsp ground cinnamon
- 3 tbsp golden caster sugar
- icing sugar, to dust

1 Heat oven to 190C/170C fan/gas 5. Lightly oil a shallow 1.3 litre baking dish. Gently heat the cherries and jam in a large pan, stirring until the jam melts over the cherries. Tip the jammy cherries into the dish and sprinkle with the lemon zest and juice.
2 Whizz the flour, eggs, milk, cinnamon and sugar in a food processor for 30 seconds until smooth. Pour over the cherries.
3 Put the dish on a baking sheet and bake for 25–30 minutes or until the custard is set and the jam is beginning to bubble through. Dust with icing sugar and serve hot.

PER SERVING (2) 532 kcals, protein 23g, carbs 92g, fat 11g, sat fat 3g, fibre 2g, sugar 38g, salt 0.66g

Guilt-free sticky toffee puds

. . . .

Date purée replaces most of the fat in this clever recipe, hence the guilt-free title!

 1½ hours   4

- 175g/6oz pitted dried dates
- 150ml/¼ pint maple syrup, plus extra to drizzle (optional)
- 1 tbsp vanilla extract
- 2 eggs, separated
- 85g/3oz self-raising flour
- 0% Greek yogurt, to drizzle (optional)

1 Heat oven to 180C/160C fan/gas 4. Simmer the dates in 175ml/6fl oz water for 5 minutes. Tip into a food processor, add 6 tablespoons of the maple syrup and the vanilla, and blend until smooth. Transfer to a bowl and mix in the egg yolks, followed by the flour.

2 Whisk the egg whites until stiff and fold into the date mixture. Put 1 tablespoon of the maple syrup into each of four 200ml/7fl oz pudding moulds. Add the date mixture. Cover each mould tightly with foil, stand the moulds in an ovenproof dish and pour in hot water to halfway up the sides of the moulds. Cook for 1 hour, until a skewer inserted into the centre comes out clean.

3 Uncover the puddings, run a knife around the edges and invert on to plates. Drizzle over some yogurt and maple syrup, if you like, to serve.

. . . .
PER SERVING 339 kcals, protein 7g, carbs 73g, fat 4g, sat fat 1g, fibre 2g, sugar 25g, salt 0.33g

Index

Also available from BBC Books and Good Food

Try 3 issues for just £3

Subscribe to **BBC Good Food magazine** for inspired ideas, reliable recipes and practical tips for all home cooks. Whether you're passionate about cooking, or just love eating good food and trying out a few easy recipes, **BBC Good Food** is the magazine for you.

Every issue includes:

★ **Triple tested recipes**
★ **Inspiring ideas**
★ **Mouth-watering photography**
★ **PLUS** as subscriber you'll receive **exclusive covers** and subscriber only offers

Subscribe today and trial your first 3 issues of
BBC Good Food magazine for just £3*

Visit **buysubscriptions.com/goodfood**
and enter code GF101B15
Call **0844 848 3414** and quote GF101B15
(Lines open Monday to Friday 8am-8pm and Saturday 9am-1pm)

This offer is available for UK delivery addresses and by Direct Debit only. *After your first 3 issues the subscription will then continue at £18.70 every 6 issues saving 22%. Normal subscription rate is UK £47.88, Europe/EIRE £60 and rest of world £72. Offer ends 30 December 2015.